Mature Interspirituality:

Wayne Teasdale's Nine Elements—and Beyond

Mature Interspirituality:

Wayne Teasdale's Nine Elements—and Beyond

SACRED FEET

The Interfaith/Interspiritual/Trans-Theological
Publishing Imprint of Slate Branch Ashram
The Jones Educational Foundation, Inc. (JEFI)
www.jefifoundation.org

Published by SACRED FEET
The Interfaith/Interspiritual/Trans-Theological
Publishing Imprint of Slate Branch Ashram
The Jones Educational Foundation, Inc. (JEFI)
A 501 (c) 3 Not-For-Profit Corporation
P.O. Box 289, Somerset, KY 42502, USA

PHOTO CREDIT
Cover photos compliments of Jeff Genung

BOOK & COVER DESIGN
Swami Shraddhananda & Sandra Simon

Printed in the United States of America
First published 2017

The SACRED FEET Publishing Imprint
Sw. Shraddhananda, Publisher
Sandra Simon, Managing Editor

ISBN: 978-0-9915010-7-6 (Paperback)
         978-0-9915010-8-3 (Kindle)

Endorsements

A rich and compelling book, *Mature Interspirituality* presents a valuable contribution to contemporary spirituality from both masculine and feminine perspectives. It is sure to stimulate and support practitioners from many traditions.

—Mariana Caplan, Ph.D., M.F.T.
Author, *Eyes Wide Open: Cultivating Discernment on the Spiritual Path* and *Yoga & Psyche: Integrating the Paths of Yoga and Psychology for Healing, Transformation, and Joy*

Mature Interspirituality breaks through the present moment into an emerging future by offering a cosmic arrowhead for the evolution of consciousness. In the first three sections, the authors collate a balanced compendium that provides a smooth and level surface for the arrowhead to cut through the invisible barriers of history and tradition. Sections three and four address the existential need for direct experience of the divine as well as an accessible technology of the sacred. Without equivocation, this compendium provides a razor-sharp critique of religion that no longer functions and presents a new practical hermeneutic of spirituality filled with meaningful possibilities.

—Dr. Matthew Cobb aka Shuddhachittananda
Director, House of Prayer, Centerville, MN

It was a joy to receive the published contents of the Community of The Mystic Heart's Interspiritual retreat held at Slate Branch Ashram in Kentucky, April 29-May 1, 2016. In furthering the rich Interfaith heritage of Br. Wayne Teasdale, Sw. Shraddhananda has been so generous as to publish these proceedings as part of The Sacred Feet Publishing Imprint's list. To hear all these accounts of dedicated spiritual practice and sacred activism across so many traditions, and from so many varied backgrounds, helps us all serve our own teachings in the most authentic way. Br. Wayne emphasized that Interspirituality is about shared resources. Swamiji's work has added another rich volume to the growing heritage of the Interfaith/Interspiritual landscape so important to our globalizing world. A divine offering!

—Karuna, Light on Kundalini, Boulder, CO

Reading *Mature Interspirituality* is like sitting down with a group of wise, gentle, and enlightened souls coming together to share their thoughts with one aim in mind—stoking the fire of our collective relationship with the Divine. Each has something of value to impart, whether it be straight knowledge, the specifics of a particular spiritual practice, generous advice, or even heartwarming personal stories that reaffirm the joys and intense fulfillment of being on the spiritual path. This book is more than interesting, it's inspiring. It calls the reader to both deepen his or her own spiritual practice and understanding, as well as feel a certain appreciation for and kinship with others here to share the light—even if their paths look a bit different from our own. We are all on this road together, after all. And as *Mature Interspirituality* conveys, we are in some very exquisite company.

—Katy Koontz, Editor of *Unity Magazine*

In a world poised perilously at the edge of chaos, there is an authentic need for the creation of shared spiritual spaces that allow for a deeper communion between people and traditions. *Mature Interspirituality* is a collection of essays inspired by one such gathering, and its pages are a (non-sectarian) prayer for humanity. Seekers of all faiths will find a home in this collection, which documents a living movement toward a contemporary planetary spirituality. May the seeds of peace contained in these pages grow wildly!

—David Nicol, Ph.D., Director & Co-Founder, Gaiafield Project
Author, *Subtle Activism: The Inner Dimension of Social and Planetary Transformation*

At a time when religion is being grossly misused as a tool for violence, and the hunger for genuine spirituality is increasing worldwide, this collection of reflections on the Nine Elements of Interspirituality of Wayne Teasdale is a sumptuous spiritual banquet. The simplicity and humility of the contributors are evident in the sharing of personal testimonies demonstrating that good values are being translated into good deeds in a variety of ways, and there is hope for planetary transformation. The reader, who is fortunate to share in the fruits of this veritable feast, is moved to profound silence.

—Fr. Dr. Prashant Olalekar
St. Xavier's College, Mumbai, India

Since the 1960s, the Interfaith and Interspirituality movements have provided an alternative for people who rejected the structure, the rigidity, and, at times, the injustice of organized religion. But the mere rejection of traditional religion doesn't necessarily produce robust new practices and philosophies. Drawing from the work of Br. Wayne Teasdale, this work provides what it terms a "mature" Interspirituality, a framework that is both simple and ambitious, nuanced but ultimately straightforward. Its authors, serious thinkers for years in the Interfaith movement, seek to provide not a rigid set of rules, but a way to think about spirituality in a world in which old barriers are falling and in which new worldviews and practices and ways of living in community are required. *Mature Interspirituality* offers practices and ideas that can re-imagine spirituality in a world that is rapidly transforming, and offer a pathway for the practitioner to transform along with it. This book is both timely and timeless, and a must-read for those interested in the Interspirituality movement.

—Dr. Theodore Richards
Author, *The Great Re-Imagining: Spirituality in an Age of Apocalypse*

Mature Interspirituality is truly a gift to all of us involved in the world of Interspirituality. Drawing upon the work of the beloved Interspiritual pioneer Wayne Teasdale, a truly distinguished array of experts and practitioners help outline how each of us can embrace an Interspiritual way of seeing and being in the world and how together we can bring about lasting transformation for the good of our planet.

—Brandan Robertson, Executive Director, Nomad Partnerships
Author, *Nomad, A Spirituality for Traveling Light*

It was great joy to meet Wayne Teasdale in the ashram several times. It was a spiritual feast to have a dialogue with him. He lived in the mystic heart and operated from that centre. Fr. Bede Griffiths had been a spiritual guide and friend to both of us. Wayne had taken the vision of Fr. Bede one step further by proposing Interspirituality and the Nine Elements as a Code of Spiritual and Ethical Conduct for Interfaith, Interspiritual, Interspecies interaction. This is a vision for the future of our spiritual evolution which can contribute to unity and peace inside and outside in the world. The authors of this book, *Mature Interspirituality: Wayne Teasdale's Nine Elements—and Beyond*, have done a tremendous job of bringing the vision of Teasdale into focus. I, whole heartedly, recommend this book to those who look for a spirituality that builds bridges among different spiritual traditions and who look for inner unity and peace.

—Br. John Martin Sahajananda
Shantivanam Ashram, Tamil Nadu, India

Contents

Acknowledgements

Many thanks to Sandra "Chamatkara" Simon who did much of the production work on *Mature Interspirituality* in the midst of a busy life at work and at home.

Gratitude is due to Jeff Genung of Austin, Texas for sending a special package that arrived just in time for the April 2016 retreat. Its contents included the *kavi* Wayne Teasdale wore for his ordination as an Interspiritual sannyasin, rare photos of Teasdale and Fr. Bede Griffiths which grace the cover of *Mature Interspirituality*, and a copy of *Toward a Christian Vedanta* from Teasdale's library.

T.S. Pennington, for years an unsung hero in the Interspiritual Movement, stepped forward and offered to drive Dr. Kurt Johnson to Kentucky from Asheville following an important Interspiritual meeting in Atlanta.

If awards were given, the top prize for selfless service would have to go to Betty Hurley, a retreatant who went out of her way to drive Mirabai Starr to her next engagement in New York State when Starr's travel plans were disrupted by severe weather. Thank you, Betty, for your Herculean efforts.

Lastly, from the management and staff of Slate Branch Ashram, home of CMH Sannyasa and Sacred Feet Yoga, it was an honor to host the first ever CMH residential retreat. This text makes every attempt to honor differences. With all due respect for conventional forms suggested by the Associated Press and the like, we have elected to follow the organic contours of each article and allow individual traits to show through rather than edit them out. Similarly, articles by writers from the United Kingdom retain British spellings rather than being Americanized. Consistency may be efficient, but the rage for uniformity can interfere with style and voice—as well as spiritual persuasion. Thank you to all who attended for your delightful contributions.

Preface

There's much discussion these days as to what constitutes "mature" spirituality. With religions jumping continents, indigenous spiritual forms resurrecting, hybrid intersections emerging, and Gurus being toppled, it can be difficult to distinguish a legitimate spirituality from a synthetic brand invented to accommodate a wayward teacher. At the same time, the Interspiritual age offers seekers openings for exploration which can be concealed when traditional religion exercises what Dr. Kurt Johnson might call "creed over deed."

With the current spiritual terrain in mind, the Community of The Mystic Heart (CMH) decided to host a retreat designed to offer seekers a grid by which to examine individuated spiritual teachings and practices. For our guiding light, we needed look no further than our own lineage to a text written by Br. Wayne Teasdale who actually coined the term "Interspirituality" with publication of *The Mystic Heart* in 1999.

"...mystical spirituality is the origin of the world's religions," Teasdale wrote. "If this is so, and I believe it is, we might say that interspirituality—the sharing of ultimate experiences across religions—is the religion of the third millennium" (MH, 26).

While Teasdale did not capitalize interspirituality in his originating definition, we have elected to cap this germinal word throughout our commentaries, because it has grown from being an important idea in Teasdale's mind into an international movement. To leave Interspirituality uncapped in our text would constitute a failure to recognize that the Interspiritual Age has, indeed, arrived.

Teasdale offered "Nine Elements" by which any spirituality could be examined for durability. One "spiritual technology," a digital-age term, might be strong on ethics, but weak in terms of the efficacy of its practices. Another might have strong practices, but turn a blind eye to a sense of right and wrong. Still another might be rich in symbols and rituals, but lacking in ways to promote heartfelt interaction. A "mature" spirituality, or Interspirituality in Teasdale's view, would integrate all "Nine Elements."

The "Nine Elements" form such a complete system that some spiritual practitioners adopt them as vows. A vow is a sacred pledge by which a seeker attempts to live her or his life. When a seeker identifies as "mystic," or "spiritual but not religious," for example, the elements can offer a way of life by which to chart spiritual progress toward "maturity" while enhancing the capacity to live life ethically in the present tense.

We held the "Nine Elements" gathering at Boat Dock Road Retreat in April 2016. Boat Dock Road is located at the head of Lake Cumberland in south central Kentucky. It was the Community of The Mystic Heart's first residential meeting, and participants came from various parts of the United States as well as Canada and the United Kingdom. Both East and West coasts were represented as were the Midwest, the Southwest, and the Deep South.

Professor Wanda Dodson, Chief Nutritionist at Slate Branch Ashram for a decade, provided our delicious vegetarian meals, and we were never without a vat of chai, thanks to Rev. Chris Vasumati Deefholts who took dual Sannyas in CMH Sannyasa and the Saraswati Order during the retreat. She was given the name Swami Prakashananda which means the "bliss" (*ananda*) of the "shining light" (*prakash*) when translated from the Sanskrit. For the initiation ceremony held at Slate Branch Ashram, the Preceptor (Sw. Shraddhananda or Mataji) wore Br. Wayne Teasdale's tomato-red Sannyasin garment, a gift from Jeff Genung of Austin, Texas, where many of Teasdale's books are housed. Professor Dodson and Sw. Prakashananda were assisted by Betty Dunz who is probably the best worker this side of the Mississippi River. She never fails to amaze when it comes to taking care of the ashram.

Fr. Giles Spoonhour, or Yeshuanananda, was ordained as a Sacred Feet Yoga Acharya during the retreat. Fr. Giles was a co-founder of The New Seminary, the oldest Interfaith seminary in the world. According to Dr. Kurt Johnson, Fr. Giles' contribution like that of other early pioneers in the Interfaith/Interspiritual/Trans-Theological Movement has been "enormous."

Dr. Darrol Bryant was present at the retreat as well. It was an honor to host this accomplished scholar. Professor Huston Smith (1919-2016), author of *The World's Religions*, considered Dr. Bryant to be his "heir apparent." Huston Smith, of course, dared to go where not even angels or wandering mendicants feared to tread very early in his career as a pioneer in the discipline of Comparative World Religions. May Huston Smith rest in peace, knowing that his contribution opened many doors for younger teachers, scholars, and spiritual seekers. Dr. Bryant's reflections on the retreat as a lively Interspiritual seminar are included in his "Afterword" to this text.

Plans were discussed during the retreat with regard to formation of Interspiritual Monks in the World (ISMW), a prong to compliment CMH Sannyasa. ISMW is now up and running and is described in detail on the CMH website. May both prongs of CMH flourish, since CMH by another name was the initial brain child of Br. Wayne Teasdale.

The lead presentations offered by Dr. Kurt Johnson, Mirabai Starr, and yours truly are included in this collection along with other interesting presentations and articles written after participants returned home and had time to digest their experiences. As you read the commentaries, organized in triads as were the lead presentations, with a fourth added here to accommodate practical implications, you may find yourself drawn to the "Nine Elements" which unfailingly distinguish Wayne Teasdale as one of the most "mature" Interspiritual thinkers of Postmodern times. Follow your intuition, and let *The Mystic Heart* fall open to virtually any page. You most likely will find what you are seeking there.

Sw. Shraddhananda
Retreat Master, "The Nine Elements of
Mature Interspirituality"

I. Morality, Solidarity, Nonviolence

Element 1: Actual Moral Capacity

Element 2: Solidarity with All Living Beings

Element 3: Deep Nonviolence

Bridging the Gap between Values and Actions by Means of Solidarity

Rev. Dr. Sw. Shraddhananda

Welcome. Welcome to the "Nine Elements of Mature Interspirituality" Retreat. Welcome to Kentucky. May you have an enjoyable stay, and may you be both challenged and strengthened to think and feel in greater depth about what it means to be a "seasoned" practitioner of Interspirituality.

My name is Sw. Shraddhananda, and I volunteered to go first among the lead presenters—Mirabai Starr and Dr. Kurt Johnson, the other two, are here with us this morning—because I have recently published a book on killing.

Killing? you may ask, raising your eyebrows. What a way to open a retreat in this beautiful setting with the floor to ceiling windows featuring the green world outside! Surely, Sw. Shraddhananda, you don't want us to take on such a brutal topic at 9 a.m. before some of us have even had coffee! Come on.

When I remind you, beloveds, you most likely will remember that Br. Wayne Teasdale's first of "nine elements," the topic of our retreat, deals with what he calls "actualizing" a "moral capacity." What could be more relevant to a sense of ethics, to any system of right and wrong, than the subject of killing—especially in an age when we lose 30,000 people in the United States alone each year to gun violence?

If it helps to ease your mind, please understand: *A Short Book about Killing* was not a text I wanted to write. I fussed, and I quit several times in the process. But, each time I walked away from the computer, another killing hit the news, and I was drawn back to the topic by a force much larger than "me." As Mirabai might say, this was a "hard book to write." And, I hear you: killing is a very difficult topic to face head-on.

Given that the so-called "great literature" of all human culture is filled with battles and family members as well as lovers lining up against each other, it can be no accident that all the world's major religious traditions inveigh against taking another human life. "No killing," the first Buddhist precept, did not find its way into Lord Buddha's recommendations for peaceful living, because the people of his time were decidedly gentle. He laid out the Noble Eight-fold Path and the Five Precepts as ways for human beings to contain their aggressive instincts.

It is unfortunately true, beloveds, that there's evidence to suggest we are killers by nature. At the same time, acts of great love and compassion continue to be recorded in the ledger of the human race. As the poet Robert Browning said, we are "wonderfully" and "fearfully" made.

In addition to Buddhism, virtually all the world's major religious traditions sanction against killing. In Judeo-Christianity, "Thou Shalt Not Kill" is the sixth commandment Moses allegedly brought down from a mountain top on a stone tablet. Many places in the United States today will not allow the "10 Commandments" to be posted, and the county in which we are retreating right now went to the Supreme Court to try and win legal permission to post these commandments in the county courthouse downtown. But, no commentator on any of the major networks, at least within my hearing distance, has mentioned this commandment in relation to the plethora of domestic and terrorist killings we have witnessed recently. Reporters could be concerned about infringing upon the separation between church and state.

As you may know, the highest court in the land ultimately ruled the "10 Commandments" could be posted as long as they appeared next to commandments from the other world religions. Not a bad ruling—an Interspiritual ruling, in fact.

What we call Hinduism, the oldest religion in the world next to Zoroastrianism, foregrounds the importance of refraining from taking another life in its legal book known as *The Laws of Manu*. Murder is considered to be the "worst" ethical offense—another reason to confront the issue of killing early in our retreat. Hinduism, actually a conglomeration of Indian spirituality, so named by the British, also places a fair amount of emphasis on the concept and practice of *ahimsa*, or hurt no living thing, which originated with the Jains.

When I first encountered the practice of *ahimsa* in a class on the world's religions in college, I thought it was the greatest thing since biscuits and gravy, a delicacy in south central Kentucky. It's no wonder, I thought, that Mahatma Gandhi placed as much emphasis on *ahimsa* in his efforts to chase the British out of India as he did on nurturing the baby goats in his *ashram*, a simple Sanskrit word meaning "sacred space."

We had goats here, too, and we have had a hard time keeping them inside fences. Goats are like Interspirituals. They do not like to be hemmed in by artificial boundaries.

The *Quran*, the scripture dear to Muslims, also urges respect for human life, although it is the most problematic of the major scriptural texts, because of the position it takes on killing the "heathen." According to ISIS, a group which would have us believe in the legitimacy of its Islamic affiliation, you and I are "the heathen," and we need to be obliterated for the prophecy of the apocalypse to be fulfilled.

Of course, no educated Muslims living in the West, or for that matter in Cairo or Istanbul, would advocate gunning down their Christian neighbors, but ISIS and other terrorist groups have latched onto language in the *Quran* which seemingly supports their ideology. *Seemingly* is the operative word here. Ideology is powerful, and it can lead human beings to overlook the fact that red blood spills from a body who is targeted as a "heathen" when he or she is shot with a military rifle known as an A-15, also called "America's gun."

In the interests of time, my intent is not to dwell on the ethics that show up in the world's religions, but to highlight the need for their existence as did Wayne Teasdale. I encourage you to have a look for yourselves. In thinking about ethics, we might get irritated sometimes with the Christian emphasis on "sin," which derives from the Latin "synne," a term from archery meaning "to miss one's mark." But, as Teasdale knew, I think, ridding ourselves of "sin," and the weight it can create internally in the form of karmic imprints lodged in the subtle body, is an important part of the purification process. Purification is necessary to climb higher into the mystic realms.

If we are looking for culprits, we could blame Hollywood, Bollywood, and the movies for spewing bloody images. We could blame the countless episodes of violence on TV. Indeed, it is difficult not to see both movies and television as strong accomplices in the culture of killing— even if we are intent on preserving artistic freedom. Admittedly, I wonder sometimes if the actor who played the lead in *Natural Born Killers*, for instance, ever experiences a pang of regret for having accepted that role. How might it feel to be a "role model" for the Columbine teenagers who blew up their high school in Colorado?

When I threatened to abandon research for a book on killing, I hasten to add, it was a filmmaker who inspired me to continue as something larger than "me" drove the "me" who resisted back to the computer. *A Short Book about Killing* pays tribute to the late Krzysztof Kieslowski who directed a 10-part series called the *Decalogue*, loosely based on the "10 Commandments." I had the good fortune to attend the American premier of the *Decalogue*, originally made for Polish television, at the San Francisco International Film Festival some twenty-five years ago. Kieslowski's work stayed with me as only great art films on par with those made by Ingmar Bergman can do.

Released from the *Decalogue* as a feature-length film, "A Short Film about Killing" served as inspiration for my book. Prophetic in its depiction of what the media has come to identify as the "lone wolf killer," Jacek Lazar, Kieslowski's protagonist, wanders the streets of Warsaw in search of meaning and purpose for his life. Instead, he finds a taxi driver to strangle.

The term, "lone wolf killer," may be offensive to animal rights activists who know that the wolf is an intelligent, highly social creature—and tends to mate for life. Native Americans see divinity in the wolf who is frequently misrepresented as a terrorist. Demeaning our fellow beings from the wild can only harm human attempts to rescue the planet from the profiteers who see no divinity anywhere, not even in the coveted dollar which is a form of living energy if regarded with integrity. As my Guru once said, it is not the four-legged creature that concerns me; it is the two-legged creature.

Jacek is an anti-hero in the tradition of Meursault

from Albert Camus's *L'Étranger* or *The Stranger.* He represents the underbelly of civilization into which "wildness" is repressed. He gives credence to Sigmund Freud's claim in *Civilization and its Discontents* that civilization itself is no less a factor in the production of darkness than are its cultural products, movies and TV.

Sigmund Freud was famous for naming what we now call the ego (sense of me), id (unconscious mind), and super-ego (sense of right and wrong created by family and culture). Freud named the super-ego last, and that probably should come as no surprise since the world Freud knew in Vienna in the 1930s was beginning to collapse as Europe succumbed to the darkness of Hitler's Third Reich— responsible for murdering some 12 million people, seven million of them Jews.

As I watch and record yet another killing in the news, I have to wonder if the psychic apparatus Freud named the super-ego is in the process of breaking down. When a society no longer consciously implants a sense of right and wrong in its young, as ours increasingly no longer does consistently, how is a sense of ethics to be formed? A spate of recent books has dealt with the rise of the psychopath, or sociopath, in Postmodern culture. Both of these labels refer to people who have diminished super-egos. Although the diagnosis appears to be accurate, I am not convinced that pathologizing people will ultimately solve the problems wrought by the loss of respect for life.

But, compassionate education might. Often, when those who have killed are tried in court—I continue to resist the word "killer," because it implies that killing is hard-wired—they express remorse for their actions. This suggests the existence of a super-ego, however rudimentary the sense of right and wrong may be. When the capacity for morality can be "actualized," as Teasdale would say, there is hope for those who have killed or committed other heinous crimes. A recent study found, in fact, that a program in California experienced a 100 percent success rate in teaching men who had killed not to kill again when they were released from prison.

One man from the study was quoted as saying that he had killed while under the influence of drugs. When he sobered up, he experienced shame. A byproduct of the super-ego, shame is a powerful agent of transformation, according to Ernest Kurtz in his book entitled *Not-God: A History of Alcoholics Anonymous*. Shame, Kurtz writes, is more effective than guilt which often passes quickly.

In alcoholics, Kurtz goes on to say, a "gap" frequently exists between the values and the behavior of the drinker. This observation can be applied to other behaviors as well. What about the stock broker, raised with a strong sense of right and wrong, who suddenly engages in a Ponzi scheme designed to rip off people's life savings? What about the husband who has been faithful to his wife for twenty years and then, seemingly without warning, asks for a divorce to marry someone with whom he has been secretly conducting an affair? What about the teenager, a Girl Scout, who is irresistibly attracted to shoplifting?

If the stock broker can put himself in the position of the person from whom he is stealing, he might be tempted to give the money he has stolen back. If the husband can get outside his "woundings" long enough to step inside his wife's pain, he might call off the affair. If the teenager can imagine being caught and hauled off to jail, while her friends jeer at her, laughing, the thrill of stealing might lose its appeal. In each of these instances, if the "gap" between values and behavior can be closed, or bridged, then the person has a shot at transformation.

How might we get inside the "gap" and assist other beings to "go to the bridge" without accusing them of being "sinners?" Historically, the religions have tried to induce shame for unacceptable actions, quite simply because shame-induced transformation is one way to address the "gap" effectively. In an age when Interspirituals are interested in the evolution of consciousness, however, punishment for committing "sins" has lost much of its appeal.

Teasdale admits to a category he calls "beyond morality," and while there does, indeed, appear to be such a state of consciousness from which morality actualizes naturally, it can also be used to justify behavior which harms other beings. It may be helpful to learn how to discern between a truly evolved being, one who integrates Teasdale's "Nine Elements," and a performance artist.

Take the "sin" of adultery, mentioned above, one of the "10 Commandments." Who takes this commandment seriously anymore? For many people, there is no "gap" to bridge here. The "sin of adultery" appears to be dropping out of the Postmodern super-ego's basket of dos and don'ts. Entertaining the senses has become increasingly more important than living a good life.

Then, there's the matter of calling virtually every sexual behavior in the field of intimate interaction "Tantric." Actually, Tantra is much larger than sex, although Eros can play an important part in the awakening of the Holy Spirit, or Maha Kundalini Shakti. Sexual pleasure is fleeting. I know. I used to be terribly interested in the full-bodied orgasm, but as a monastic, I am more committed now to the "cessation of desire" and to celibacy as helpmates in the dance toward spiritual "maturity."

Do I think that householders are capable of attaining "Interspiritual maturity?" Absolutely not. I think everyone of you here today should take monastic vows while you are in residence in Kentucky. Teasing. Testing to see if you are awake. Of course, householders are just as capable of attaining "Interspiritual maturity" as monastics are. And, it's almost time for morning break. Soon, you will be able to phone home to let your significant others know you arrived here safely.

There is a way to "bridge the gap" between values and behavior. It's in the second of Wayne Teasdale's "Nine Elements:" "Solidarity with all living beings." If we focus on the "interconnectedness of everyone and everything" (MH, 114), then surely it would become harder for us to spray bullets into a crowd of innocent people.

Cultivating "solidarity with all living beings" means developing a sense of empathy. If we can take the position of "the other" who is different from us, then it becomes harder to see him or her as a threat, an enemy, or a "heathen." As my late mother used to say, "Do not criticize the Indian until you have walked a mile in his moccasins." Empathy helps to lessen the temptation to be judgmental of others.

In *A Short Book about Killing*, I included a final chapter entitled, "Letter to a Jihadist from a Heathen." I took the inspiration for this letter from Ranier Maria Rilke's "Letter to a Young Poet" which I taught many times in my former life as an English professor before I became a professor of Comparative World Religions. My "Letter to a Jihadist" was written directly after the San Bernardino massacre when several people were slaughtered by a radicalized couple whose ideology prompted them to deposit their baby with a relative and seek revenge on co-workers at a Christmas party in southern California. In my "Letter," I took the position of the "heathen."

Were I to take the position of those who killed, I would say (and have said): "I do not understand you. I feel wounded by the 'American infidel' who tried to 'occupy' my land. I am angry. I want to strike back. I want to create a place for our caliphate, our heaven on earth. You do not even know what a caliphate is."

Problem is: ideology is a drug as strong as heroin, and the "heathen" is also trying to create a heaven on earth. Virtually all societies are enamored of "the city on the hill," and we all tend to believe that everything will be okay on planet earth if we can put our Utopian ideas into practice. Even Adolf Hitler committed suicide in a bunker after trying to create a Master Race which meant murdering millions of Jews he believed to be too inferior to exist in his Utopia.

Dearly beloved participants in the first international meeting of the Community of The Mystic Heart, I submit to you: if we focus on cultivating a sense of solidarity instead of driving a wedge between ourselves and other human beings, we can learn to live in a state of "deep non-violence." If we stop with ourselves, however, we can easily get stuck in a deadly self-consciousness which all too often entangles us in webs of anger, greed, and lack, the internal manufacturers of egoic desire.

As Wayne Teasdale wrote, "Spiritual maturity is not about pursuing salvation alone; it is about contributing to the salvation or enlightenment of others" (MH, 113).

The Nine Elements of Animal Assisted Chaplaincy: Notes Toward Efficacy and Ethically Responsible Interspecies Interactions

Rev. Elizabeth Teal

On a beautiful day in the Spring of 2016, I found myself driving to a retreat in the Kentucky hills. I was given what appeared to be clear instructions. My husband had even written them in color-coded ink. Of course, as was so often the case when there were clear instructions in life, I got lost. Having been lost so often in my life, however, I now never get *hopelessly* lost. There are simply too many avenues of assistance, but I am occasionally late...

I set off with the intention of arriving at Slate Branch Ashram shortly after lunch, but I was quickly disabused of that idea. Seeing the road I was traveling on disintegrate into a construction site, I realized that literally there was no more road! Turning around, I found a small detour sign and ended up back in Tennessee at a small truck stop, currently out of unleaded gasoline. They had diesel and directions, but I needed unleaded gas, so off I drove in the opposite direction. After several more wrong turns, and after meeting several more very helpful people and one truly lovely soft black dog, I arrived—in the dark—just in time to be whisked down to Boat Dock Road Retreat to catch the end of dinner.

It was delicious and warm, and I could eat everything offered, which is rare, as I do not consume the animals of land or sky—part of vows I took long ago, vows that are still relevant as I commit myself more deeply to living a life guided by universal principles of faith in action.

How we eat says so much about how we live in balance on this planet.

My meditation that night took me over the hills and valleys before me, and reminded me of those I had just traveled as the owls hooted their wisdom from the sweet-smelling trees. Part of my daily practice is an ink brush meditation on the day at hand along with my interactions with other species. When I have internet access, I post the paintings and words on a blog at MinistryofAnimals.org, but tonight, I simply prayed and painted, meditated and dreamed, as the world wide web at Slate Branch Ashram was more like Indra's net.

I fell asleep in the loft at State Branch, listening to the wind running through the trees. This space, this place felt blessed and holy. Morning came softly.

Although I took Wayne Teasdale's Nine Elements from *The Mystic Heart* as vows in 2011, this is the first retreat I have attended that focuses on "The Nine Elements of Mature Spirituality." I am surprised not to see familiar faces, and the one face I know doesn't recognize me. But, there is nothing unusual in that. Briefly, I ponder my maturity, and I introduce myself.

"I am Elizabeth Teal, an Interfaith Interspiritual minister. I am ordained through One Spirit Interfaith Seminary. My field is in the interconnection of all life, and how that heals, helps and holds us in wholeness. I am a spiritual director for The Ministry of Animals and a specialist in sacred ceremony, divine creativity and what is usually called the 'human-animal' bond."

Or perhaps, that is what I wish I had said, so I am saying it to you now, dear reader!

In 2009, I became very attracted to the work of Br. Wayne Teasdale and the term he coined: *Interspirituality*. In that work, he identified nine components, or parts, that active participants in religious life, or seekers of faith, have in common. I was so enchanted with the simplicity and relevance of this list that I took them as vows when I became a member of the Community of The Mystic Heart. Inevitably, they figured into my Interspecies ministry.

I have been involved with "Animal Assisted Activities," "Animal Assisted Therapies" and "Animal Assisted Education" for over 30 years—often known in the media as the catch-all categories of "Pet Therapy" using "Therapy Dogs."

I have been involved in "Animal Assisted Crisis" and "Trauma Response" since the terms first began to appear in 2001. My Cavalier King Charles Spaniel Annie and I were the first team called into the "Family Assistance Pier" for children survivors. We continued there until it closed. My experiences partnering with first responders and mental health workers left a real need, un-named and untrained—a need I was seeing filled, almost by accident, it seemed, by the presence of well-trained Dog/Handler Visiting Teams. As I progressed as a Trainer/Behavior Specialist, I began to experience more and more of the possibilities that come with working in harmony with other species towards our human health and overall well-being; as I progressed spiritually, I began to experience a unity of purpose beyond what I had words or examples for…a need being filled in ancillary ways while we were unaware.

That need was literally the holding of Sacred Presence, in the reality of the moment, sans story. Now, my other vocation is that of storyteller. I create and tell original stories and a series of mythologies for the emerging age, and I am a huge proponent of the healing powers of story. As an active teller, I believe we are the storytelling animal, but I no longer believe it is the only tool needed in our medicine pouch! In fact, the other essential tool is its direct opposite—the healing power of no-story—the healing power of Sacred Presence.

After the events of 9-11, New York City was like a raw open emotional wound; even as the rest of the country and world was grappling with the meaning and shift of identities, New Yorkers were dealing with immediate family loss, income loss, and a new found fear of blue skies. Annie and I were downtown at what was called "Ground Zero" as part of the Red Cross Mental Health Teams traveling with the New York Police Department. It was a crime scene, after all.

We were walking to the staging platform from the ferry. I was carrying Annie since the ground was too toxic for me to put her feet down. Annie and I were walking beside a small elderly woman whose shoulders were visibly shaking as she walked. A large handsome blond white man came up on her other side and leaned down to comfort her. He was clad in a sparkling white uniform with a sparkling gold cross. Just then, I saw the tiniest Star of David on a thin golden chain at her throat as she suddenly looked at him and recoiled as if receiving an electric shock.

She wheeled into me, enveloping my little canine partner. Time seemed to freeze. Everything was bright white, glowing for a moment, an eternity. Sound came suddenly flooding in as if to remind me that everything had been soundless and beyond quiet. And there was this woman cradling my dog. EMTs were running over as she calmly looked up at me, and our eyes locked for a moment.

"This was not God's will," she said, letting go of me, gesturing at the destruction. "This is, life is…" and she held Annie for the rest of the trip. When we disembarked the ferry back uptown, she said, 'Thank you." We simply held each other's eyes and hearts for a moment before she walked back onto dry land wet with tears.

Stories like these started to pile up around 9-11, occurrences where there were no words, but an amazing grace, a knowing accompanied by feelings of the deepest love.

Another plane crashed. It made only small headlines, local headlines. Mechanical malfunctions compounded by pilot error, or some say vice versa—an accident, perhaps—this crash appeared only as a footnote, *except to those who lost loved ones and or livelihoods*. And it was there that the seeds of Animal Assisted Chaplaincy were firmly planted in my psyche. I was visiting with a young child whose grandmother had died on that plane. She was sitting on a big plastic chair with her legs dangling, looking grey and listless. Annie practically leapt out of my arms into her lap. I stopped and, as always, asked permission, "Would you like a visit from a dog?"

Above her head, a silver figure appeared. I looked back into the girl's eyes. They were almost hollow, and against protocol (you are supposed to always get a "yes confirmation signal" from the subject), I gently placed Annie into her lap. Suddenly, the girl appeared to be surrounded by what can only be described as light beings, angels, and what seemed to me to be ancestors and relatives. The color came back into her cheeks, her eyes came to light, and she began babbling away in Spanish to the little spaniel. We all stayed this way for quite some time, until someone came to pick her up. I never knew her name, nor have I ever told anyone this particular story, but it changed my commitment to what I know is possible.

My work in Interspirituality is most accurately a

direct outgrowth of my work with other species. From animal training for communication, to animal assisted activities of all sorts, to the simple grace of companionship, I have seen the Holy in action. It was and is in this capacity that I felt called to create ways and means for responsible partnering with other species toward human recovery, rehabilitation and quality of life. For me as an Interspiritual minister, this naturally became the groundwork for Animal Assisted Chaplaincy (AAC).

Out of my experiences during 9-11 and several other incidents afterward, I recommitted myself to both interspecies relationships and to deeper explorations of spirituality, both personally as well as historically. Out of this commitment came a holistic approach to partnering with other species in times of both spiritual exploration (Animal Assisted Spiritual Direction and Eco-Ministry) and in times of crisis and trauma (Animal Assisted Chaplaincy and Eco-Chaplaincy). These new fields are still very much in flux with standards of practice being defined even as I write this...and it is my hope to help provide a basis for responsible and ethical platforms as this field develops.

Since concepts of mature spirituality are integral to ethical chaplaincy, I was very excited about the Nine Elements retreat. And the meditations and thought forms that it produced have affected my life and work in too many ways for one article. Therefore, I have narrowed the focus to Animal Assisted Chaplaincy as it is very new in this world. Animal Assisted Chaplaincy is the partnering with other species by trained Chaplains to provide sacred listening and create holy spaces in and at times of trauma, crisis and uncertainty.

It is not simply the arrival of a happy friendly dog at one end of a leash, and the dog is not some magical chaplain providing unconditional love. In fact, the myth that "animals provide unconditional love" or that they "love unconditionally" does more damage to the huge potential of Animal Assisted Chaplaincy than, perhaps, any other myths that surround interspecies interactions. It is not only too huge a burden to bear, it is so readily exposed, that those for whom this myth is dear, find themselves in deep inauthenticity, creating stories to cover natural behaviors and overriding real-time stress responses in both the clients and the animal partners, not to mention the handlers. Animal Assisted Chaplaincy is about providing authentic sacred presence, sans dogma or creed, in faith or lack thereof. Well-done AAC is Interspirituality in action.

Looking at the Nine Elements identified by Br. Wayne Teasdale as being the common core elements of all religious seeking/seekers, I find a useful framework to apply to a wide variety of religious and/or sacred vocations. They can provide a guidance template for further development, as well as a bedrock in which to ground our ethical behaviors and our paths partnering with other species.

I hope to provide a useful tool, a rubric of sorts by which to gauge growth and efficacy as the Human half of an Animal Assisted Chaplaincy Team. The goal of Animal Assisted Chaplaincy, in general, is the assisting of human beings in distress, trauma and transition. The goal of this exercise is not to replace any vows, or principles. The main action of responsible chaplaincy is the active holding of sacred presence and holy listening. This is, of course, impossible unless both elements of the Chaplaincy team are willing and mindful, but here I am only addressing the human half of the team.

These are the daily intentions I have cobbled together from the work of Br. Wayne in his book, *A Monk in the World.* Here they are in third person; I invite you to write them into first person, using your name as you ask yourself, "How can I do that today?" "What does that look like in this moment?"

For example, using the First Element: "An Interfaith Interspiritual Interspecies Chaplain strives to actualize and live according to her or his personal moral and ethical capacity," I might write, adding, "I, Elizabeth Teal, strive today to actualize and live according to my personal moral and ethical capacity by reading (whatever current book); by journaling today's experiences; by (list an action of the day such as cleaning the house, training a new dog, visiting XYZ facility, writing a Congressperson, etc.); by seeing You in every face I encounter; by listening to and trying to understand rather than interjecting; and by giving thanks repeatedly, as I remind myself of my astounding blessings as I listen to You."

So often with the best intentions, I think, we want to make commitments, and then realize they feel too big, too unattainable, and so we drop the entire intention! I urge all of us in this undertaking to think of each element as a simple step—each one marking a new moment—each one a step we take again and again, spiraling gently upwards.

The Nine Elements as a Code of Spiritual and Ethical Conduct for Interfaith Interspiritual Interspecies Chaplain

1. An Interfaith Interspiritual Interspecies Chaplain strives to actualize and live according to her or his personal moral and ethical capacity.

2. An Interfaith Interspiritual Interspecies Chaplain strives to respect and live in holy community with *all* living beings—regardless of species, gender, gender identity, age, creed, sexual orientation, personal identification, nationality, status, or history. In this context, acknowledging that "all" has often meant "all like me," we are mindful that we have blind spots, as we strive toward clear sightedness. All means All.

3. An Interfaith Interspiritual Interspecies Chaplain strives to live a life of nonviolence and seeks to view all training as mutual and communicative. Non-violence can, at first, seem simple, but can easily lead to a spiritual bypass when it comes to our companion animals and the foods both they and we eat, as well as the methodologies utilized to train both us and them. Thus, we must acknowledge that where our food comes from, as well as the different needs of individuals and species, causes us to promote balance and responsible farming, husbandry, hunting and reclamation of carrion for our partners as well as ourselves. All training is to be viewed as mutual communication and is to be done using the best of current science-based practices and stress reduction techniques tailored to each individual partner. Violent methodologies and the use of pain, force, or extended intentional deprivation have no place in the training of a team.

4. An Interfaith Interspiritual Interspecies Chaplain strives to live in humility and to remember the many teachers and guides who assisted, and assist them on their path, whether they have two feet or four, or are furred, feathered, finned; whether they have conferred letters after their name, or family titles. Rather than adhering

to only one ideology, school of thought, or one system of education and training, remember and honor all those that taught you, even if those lessons were lessons of avoidance while remembering moments of grace and learning. Honor those teachers whose lessons you are still assimilating. Walk humbly with teachers whose lessons you have outgrown, knowing you always have much to learn, and are always surrounded by teachers in every moment.

5. An Interfaith Interspiritual Interspecies Chaplain strives to embrace spiritual and interspecies training and communication practices daily, both as individuals and with her or his non-human partners. Daily spiritual practice for Animal Assisted Chaplaincy is both a partnered process and an individual one. Individually, we practice communicating and experiencing the Holy through prayer, meditation and acts of service; together, we practice meditation, open communication and science based behavioral training so that we, as a team are, and will be, ready to hold Sacred Presence when we are called. It is absolutely critical to practice responsibly and daily with your partner.

6. An Interfaith Interspiritual Interspecies Chaplain strives to cultivate self-knowledge as well as knowledge of her or his own human species and to know the unique individuals, the breeds and the species that are our partners.

7. An Interfaith Interspiritual Interspecies Chaplain strives to live a life of simplicity and gentleness in relation to her or his immediate surroundings, the Earth and all Her denizens. Always carry water for your team. Pick

up all refuse and dispose of it responsibly. Reduce, reuse and recycle, remembering to take no more than you will use.

8. An Interfaith Interspiritual Interspecies Chaplain strives to live a life of service and compassionate action with other species and with her or his human species—never putting one above the other, but working together to serve the greater whole.

9. An Interfaith Interspiritual Interspecies Chaplain strives to be a compassionate prophetic voice for healing, equity, and justice in all her or his actions with other species, and the human, too. We do this by the simplest of actions as well as how we choose to show up in the world.

Lest you, dear reader, think that the interactions that led me to Animal Assisted Chaplaincy have ended, leaving only difficult practice, or that they were the product of a specific special dog—although Annie certainly was that—nothing could be further from the truth...

Annie has crossed over, and I now partner with a Standard Poodle named Tomi. We find time to discover new words, to listen, and to integrate the work of the Nine Elements daily, starting our days together with my morning lauds, though I could not tell you if Tomi prays, even though every day he is with me when I meditate.

Perhaps there is no element with which we are more engaged than the third—a dedication to non-violence as a way of life—for it spills over into aspects of the other elements. It is the "compassion key" that unlocks the work we do together. Before every training session, for instance, we always check in with how we feel first, and then, we

23

adjust accordingly. "Will this be an active physical session or a quiet intellectual one?" we ask. In training, neither of us is wearing or holding a leash. Sometimes, I have a bag of treats by my side, sometimes a toy, and sometimes I don't. What do we look like as a team when we visit?

Before we leave, I ask Tomi if he wants to go, and he almost always dances his little dance straight to the door. Only once did he go into the bedroom instead. We canceled our visit, and he later had diarrhea and threw up.

Tomi wears a harness and leash. I view them like seat belts in cars. They are for safety. They are not the engine, nor the steering wheel. I have a bag at my waist with my "smart phone," (it has prayers and sacred texts on it), as well as a camera, my ID, some cookies, a comb, wet ones, Silver Shield gel (a disinfectant) biodegradable poop bags, and water. And, we set off. Upon arriving at a facility, we sign in and then proceed to go wherever we have been called. I never know quite where that will be. Most often, we go and sit with whomever we are called to. Sometimes we pray together, or meditate. Occasionally, we sing, and we always start out humbly. "Would you like a visit from a dog?" we ask, entering any situation with respect.

Last Fall we were asked to visit a residential rehab facility, but when we got there, the room we were to use was filled with a craft activity. We were asked to wait. We agreed. While waiting, Tomi started to pull me into another area. I looked at him as if to say, "Patience, you know we walk on loose leads," and he threw his head at me! So, I asked him where he needed to go, and I followed. The leash loose, we quietly walked up to a woman who was in a wheelchair, and he nuzzled her hand. She opened her eyes and started to pet his head. Then she took his paw and kept stroking it. As he looked at her, she began to cry. Soft gentle tears. I simply held the space. No words were being spoken. Slowly, I realized a circle had formed around us. She looked up at me and told me it was "okay for me to go now." I said, "thank you," and as we were leaving, a man I passed was saying that he didn't know how he was going to tell the woman in the wheelchair her dog had just passed that morning. I knew she already knew...which indeed she did.

The practicing of the Nine Elements simply provides a framework to contain, to connect, and to hold, if you will, the Holy—however you define it, however you wish to grow with it.

I want to close by acknowledging the fullness of working with all of the elements, as well as the richness that I believe this work gives to your own unique spiritual expressions. I leave you with my meditation the night I drove back from the retreat—a meditation that encompasses the second element and the ninth.

Evolution
Posted on May 3, 2016 by eteal

Driving on a ribbon of road,
i contemplate the change/flow.
i find a tick on my garments at a rest stop,
and vows of non-violence
become co-mingled with thoughts of diseases.
Suddenly
a giant spider jumps into my focus.
I grip the steering wheel tighter—
my animal awarenesses on high alert...
then i see the glass,

and the metal
strewn on the pavement.
The spider—a shredded tire—
i pass under signs telling me of the human tolls on the road.
the numbers climb as i travel back home.
(no mention of the dog who has passed that i just passed on
the shoulder.)

We evolved to fear the spider,
How long til we learn to be mindful on the road?
How long til we honor all our paths?
Just then, the birds in the trees took flight.
.

II. Humility, Spiritual Practice, Mature Self-Knowledge

Element 4: Humility of Heart

Element 5: Spiritual Practice

Element 6: Mature Self-Knowledge

Cultivating Contemplative Life

Mirabai Starr

When we meet the Beloved inside the quiet garden of the heart, our natural response is to share the bounty. In the wake of such an encounter, the vessel of the soul overflows and spills into the waiting cup of the world. Cultivating a contemplative life is not an alternative to being of service; it is entwined with the impulse to serve.

In an effort to identify the essence of the "mystic character" Br. Wayne Teasdale identified nine key elements that we find across the spectrum of spiritual traditions. The development of each of these attributes leads us beyond a preoccupation with the self and energizes us to help alleviate suffering in the world. Some kind of intentional contemplative practice is vital for nurturing these qualities.

In this chapter I will be exploring the middle three elements: humility, spiritual practice, and mature self-knowledge. Drawing on my own deep connection with the Spanish mystics as a translator of John of the Cross and Teresa of Avila, I will be taking a look at these universal spiritual features through the inclusive lens of their teachings.

Humility

"The humble man or woman has chosen to be fully who they are." (Br. Wayne)

For Br. Wayne, humility is entwined with love. Motivated by a desire to respond to the needs of others, our hearts open and our egos rest. We are not speaking here about a sentimental self-deprecation, which is another form of self-absorption in disguise. True humility demands fearless self-inquiry and radical authenticity. It takes great courage to strip off our armor and walk naked onto the field of the heart.

All great spiritual traditions recognize annihilation as a necessary station of the spiritual path. In Sufism it is called *fana*, to "die before you die," and it is a prerequisite for *baqa*, union with God. In mystical Judaism the goal of prayer is to reach a state of *bitul hayesh*, "nullification of one's somethingness." The sixteenth century Indian poet, Mirabai, exclaimed, *Be ready to orbit his lamp like a moth giving in to the light…to live in the partridge that swallows hot coals for love of the moon…like a bee trapped for life in the closing of the sweet flower.* Such burning is an excruciating process, yet it is all our souls really want. Without crucifixion there can be no resurrection.

The legendary Spanish mystic, Teresa of Avila, envisioned the soul as a magnificent crystal castle at the center of which the Beloved himself abides, beckoning us to union. Our only task is to turn inward and make our way into his arms. Yet this is the most challenging journey there is, and we are thrown off course at every turn by the slithering serpents of vanity and self-righteousness. Teresa delineates seven stages of this inner journey, and the first is the same as Br. Wayne's fourth element of a mature spirituality: humility.

For Teresa, as it for Br. Wayne, humility is predicated on self-awareness. When we take an honest look at our own mental habits and sensory attachments, it is difficult to hang onto any sense of entitlement. This is not about seeing ourselves as wrong or bad. True humility, the product of uncompromising self-inquiry, strips away the superficial layers that comprise the false self and grants us direct access to the Holy. When we recognize our nothingness before the vastness of the Divine, we are paradoxically ready for union with All That Is.

This is the first step of the Buddha's Eightfold Path, "right view," which is about seeing reality as it is, rather than as we wish it was. This also means seeing ourselves as we are instead of how we'd prefer to be. When we face our own shadow it becomes difficult to maintain our self-importance. Preoccupation with our own status falls away and we become much more interested in alleviating sorrow in those around us.

Spiritual Practice

Br. Wayne considers spiritual practice to be nothing less than the technology of transformation. If humility shows us where we are stuck, spiritual practice gives us the means and the motivation to change it. This is not a self-improvement project, but rather a path of alchemical transmutation. By offering the lead of our shortcomings into the flames of prayer and meditation, we emerge with something golden and fruitful with which to feed the hungry world and offer praise to the Creator.

Spiritual methodologies such as *Lectio Divina*, Centering Prayer, mantra repetition, mindfulness, Zazen, Yoga, Tai Chi, chanting and conventional liturgy have been engineered over millennia to connect the practitioner with the source of her heart's deepest desire. The Spanish mystics speak of two stages of spiritual experience, the active and the passive. In the active stage, we cultivate a disciplined practice, sweeping out the chamber of the heart.

In the passive stage, the Holy One takes over.

In Christian mystical theology this process is known as the *Via Negativa*, and it has three stages. In the *Via Puragtiva*, we intentionally engage practices of purification, such as fasting, prayer, solitude and silence. In the *Via Iluminitiva*, the divine light comes pouring into the scoured vessel of the heart. In the *Via Unitiva*, the warmth of the divine radiance melts the container and the separate self dissolves into the Beloved.

Teresa of Avila speaks of contemplative life as "waters of prayer." At the beginning, we must drop our bucket into the deep well of prayer and haul it back up using all our might. The waters slosh over the sides of the bucket and we lose some. We lose a little more as we carry the bucket to the garden and water each seedling by hand. Later we learn to crank the water wheel and channel the flow through a series of elaborately engineered aquaducts. We dig little ditches along each row of the garden so that the waters will reach the plants we wish to tend. This is a noisy, splashy, complicated business. The best water of all is the one that comes as a gentle rain falling directly from the sky, penetrating the soil and and nourishing the plants from their roots. This is called "infused contemplation." It is grace. Teresa sometimes refers to it as the "prayer of quiet," in which all our clamoring efforts to reach the Beloved relax and the Beloved himself fills us with the deep and subtle sweetness of his presence.

Mature Self-Knowledge

"Self-knowledge is so important that I do not care how high you are raised up to the heavens, I never want you to cease cultivating it."
(Teresa of Avila)

For Br. Wayne, humility is the foundation on which we build true knowledge of the self. We can see the natural flow of energy here from humility (seeing ourselves as we are) to spiritual practice (activating transformational technologies) to mature self-knowledge (actualizing our potential for union with the Divine).

The term "mature self-knowledge" may conjure images of pious believers behaving in a sober fashion. Yet most spiritual masters have a twinkle in their eye and a playful spirit. It is joy, not grim determination, that marks a person whose heart and mind have awakened by love. It is humor, not self-righteousness, that keeps us in touch with reality and checks us when we start veering into self-absorption.

Paradoxically, mature self-knowledge also involves *unknowing*. In his mystical masterpiece, *Dark Night of the Soul*, John of the Cross makes it clear that the "spiritual adept" is someone for whom all conceptual constructs regarding ultimate reality must at some point unravel. This is the advanced version of the Dark Night, when all the ideas we used to depend on to prop up our spiritual lives reveal themselves as empty. The God we love no longer fits in the box of theology. It is by not knowing we come to know truly. Spiritual practices carry us beyond themselves. *"All ways lead finally to this place that transcends all we thought we knew before."* (Br. Wayne)

Contemplative life, Br. Wayne reminds us, changes everything. As our consciousness expands, so does our capacity for transformation. Our will naturally desires the good. Our emotions stabilize and begin to serve us on our our journey, rather than distract us. Our character is "reshaped in and by the virtues, values, and spiritual treasures of the inner journey." The imagination harmonizes with the will. The memory shifts to the "eternal now" and stops "wallowing in past hurts and traumas." Our hearts become permeable to the suffering of others and our actions line up with the desire to be of service.

Remember, a life of contemplative prayer does not rescue us from the world but rather places us squarely in the midst of the human condition where we take our rightful place in a web of belonging. *"This is what I would like us to strive for, friends,"* says Teresa of Avila. *"We should engage in prayer—thirst for it, even—not because it feels good, but because it gives us the strength we need to be of service."*

Br. Wayne would agree.

Kicking the Ego in the Can
with *Seva* and the Breath

Acharya Sandra "Chamatkara" Simon

"The eighth element of universal spirituality is love-in-action, selfless service, and compassionate response to the sufferings of others. This is the proof of the genuineness of one's spiritual life. It cannot be real without this dimension of action out of love, kindness, compassion, and sensitivity. The capacity to respond to others from the innateness of love, compassion, kindness, and sensitivity is directly related to living his or her spiritual life. The more we are immersed in the Divine Presence, or exposed to infinite Awareness, the more we become love-in-action, pure kindness, compassion, and sensitivity, and sensitivity is a vast awareness, a consciousness that transcends our human limitations. It is the inner, natural, emergent intention of the person with a good heart, a perfected being, a holiness of life."—Wayne Teasdale

For as far back as I can remember, my prayer to God growing up as a child was simply, "God, make me good. Really, really good." I wanted to be kind. I wanted to be love. I wanted to do "good" and do what was right. In my heart, I wanted to come from a place of love and goodness in everything that I did. I never wanted to be "bad."

I also was taught at an early age to offer my hands and help for whatever was needed by others and to do it with a smile and positive attitude, and furthermore, actually feel positive down to my heart about it (i.e., not to look at it as something for which you just put on a happy face but inside were miserable to help). In life, of course, some self-less service is easier than others to do while feeling completely positive about it, and I think, the goal is to get to the state all the time where you act from a place of love, and feel that love down to your core while you offer yourself and your gifts up to another. What helps this, of course, is having compassion for others and their circumstances and feeling that oneness with others so that offering your assistance to them feels like offering assistance to yourself, but that takes time to develop and maintain.

As I grew, I found historically that it was easier to maintain "goodness" and a loving, kind disposition and to offer seva (selfless service) when I was in an intimate relationship with the divine and beseeching the sacred for those gifts through grace. I remember praying, vividly, in tears, on numerous occasions (and not just in early childhood) for God to grant me every virtue on the planet and make me good. As a child, obviously, I didn't recognize exactly what I was doing or that it was the Eighth Element of universal spirituality, but it always felt right to me.

Now, as an adult, I practice Sacred Feet Yoga, an Interspiritual Yoga, and I am very conscious in my own personal sadhana that I have been honing the Eighth Element of universal spirituality all of my life. While all of the Sacred Feet Teachings contribute to being "good," or having a universal spiritual consciousness in tune with the divine, there are certain parts of The Teachings of Sacred Feet Yoga that specifically tie into the Eighth Element and help me to be compassionate, to be love-in-action, to be kind, and to offer seva.

The First Teachings kindle love-in-action, kindness and compassion for others and also for myself, invoking the thought process of interconnectedness in how we treat others and ourselves, and offering up the virtues that we can practice or enact so that we can treat each other and ourselves with love, kindness and respect, getting us on the path to line up and act in accordance with the divine, as Kurt Johnson has said, becoming a best friend with our Self. Sometimes, for me, when the concept of God or the sacred gets too big, it helps to focus on these virtues to regroup and ground myself back into an intimate relationship of being one with the divine in kindness, compassion, love and the rest of the divine virtues. The First Teachings of Sacred Feet Yoga are:

Be as kind to yourself as you are compassionate to others.
Be as forgiving of yourself as you are generous with others.
Be as patient with yourself as you are faithful to others.

Plainly, for me, The Fourth Teachings address attitude and seva. They remind me of my childhood lesson of lend a hand with a happy heart. These teachings have worked for me all of my life, even before I had them spelled out for me in Sacred Feet Yoga in an Interspiritual way, and I've always been called "good help" by family and friends. Being "good help" just takes on a whole other dimension and meaning when taken into the context of Interspiritual advocacy and personal sadhana. The Fourth Teachings are:

Live your life peacefully—and with purpose.
Maintain a glad sense of humor.
Place your faith in stillness, steadiness, and service.

I find, as I grow and experience the divine in my sadhana, acting from a place of love and offering seva becomes ever more and more important. As an Acharya of Sacred Feet Yoga, I have the calling to live and teach the Sacred Feet Teachings to others. One must practice what one teaches, of course, but even more than that, I am connecting my Self to others in this manner, becoming one with people in love, kindness and seva. Growing up, it was a solitary wish to be "good" and an independent thing to be "good help." I now see that it is a way to connect across spiritual traditions, and beyond.

In Sacred Feet Yoga, this principle is very much in practice...to welcome those of all spiritual traditions, or none, and to meet each other in our good works, in our respectful and enriching discussions, in our love and respect for each other, and in our dedication to promote a world with people consistently living, responding, participating and giving from the highest Self, thus raising the sacred vibration of the whole and changing the world in which we live so that there is not separation or "otherness" and the severe things that result when we are operating from the ego's facets of individual desire and fear, such as killing.

Pope Francis said that "doing good" is a principle that unites all humanity, beyond the diversity of ideologies and religions, and it creates the "culture of encounter" that is the foundation of peace. He said that, if we meet there, each doing our own part, doing good, and we go slowly, gently, little by little, we will make that culture of encounter: we need that so much. We must meet one another "doing good." Go to:

http://en.radiovaticana.va/storico/2013/05/22/pope_at_mass_culture_of_encounter_is_the_foundation_of_peace/en1-694445

In a recent video I saw posted on Facebook, I was reminded of just how much you can accomplish together, regardless of personal differences. A man was emotionally recounting a family (of another ethnicity than him) who bought an overgrown, abandoned house next door to him. On the day the house sold, the new owner showed up with nine trucks of workers. Those workers worked all night long. In the morning, much to the man's astonishment, the house was completely remodeled and ready for the family to move into it. It looked "brand new." The man said to the new neighbor, "What kind of crew you got working after 7:00?" The neighbor said, "These are my friends!" At this point in the video, the man passionately broke down. He called into action his own community. He said that he was looking forward to seeing what his neighbors were going to do next, and he was planning to get to know his neighbors. He also said that when he made some money that he was going to work to bring people together.

I was moved by this story for several reasons. First, it shows how seva, truly selfless service, can build something—accomplish something for the betterment of a person or society. Second, it shows that seva reaches people mentally and emotionally across those boundaries or divides that exist because of our differences to foster respect and understanding. Last, it shows that seva inspires more seva, forging common ground in doing good, fostering that culture of encounter and inclusion, despite what our differences may be. Simply, doing "good" works to bring people together and to make us better versions of ourselves. It gets us out of our egos and the "I, me, mine" mindset and gets us to start thinking collectively and about things beyond our own personal needs and wants.

Further, you can be amazed at what personal results

that seva ends up having on you, spiritually and otherwise. Often, when a person is having a problem or a difficult time and can't think herself out of it or work through something, if she asks me what to do, I'll tell her to go do seva. Just go do something for someone else. It doesn't matter what, just go do some good work. It is uncanny how you can get yourself personally "unstuck" by giving of yourself in seva. It gets you up and out of the ego so that you can reconnect with the inner Self.

Personally, one of my latest seva assignments has been to function as Managing Editor for The Sacred Feet Publishing Imprint. Swami Shraddhananda's *A Short Book About Killing* has been the latest offering from our publishing house to the Interspiritual world. As Dr. Joni Dittrich, aka Kalisara, mentioned in her review on Amazon, "The author reveals the hypocrisy and idiocy of much of the nation's thinking about killing and helps us to look at how we may express outrage one day and seem to accept the outrageous as part of the norm the next. Not an easy subject to think about, but so important and timely. Or, perhaps, unfortunately, timeless." As Dr. Kurt Johnson said in his review, "In these polarizing times, *A Short Book about Killing* offers wisdom, compassion, and hope." To perform seva in a way that facilitates the offering of work that is intended to address the current problems in society and endeavors to reach out to people of all spiritual traditions to find common ground is very humbling and, indeed, enriching. People often ask, "What can I do in the face of the world's ills?" I feel like offering this seva, playing a small part in bringing people together in conversations stemming from the highest Self, is me doing something, utilizing some of my gifts from grace to contribute to work that is aiming to raise Consciousness so that people are responding from the highest *matrika,* or linguistic level of speech and print.

Not that it has been easy like Sunday morning, of course. Let me be clear on that. Sometimes seva challenges us, and sometimes, it challenges us to a level that nothing else can. Seva asks us to stretch and reach and grow into our talents, dig deep into the Self, and give up the ego. I never in my life made a book before. I never navigated the technical side of creation or the process of getting it marketed and distributed. I pretty much started with a blank page and said to myself, as I often do, "What is the worst that can happen?" I had no idea what I was in for, as they say. But, I figured that I would give it a try with a clear heart and open mind and see just what I could do, beseeching the divine for help, of course. I also figured that, if nothing else, I would learn something about myself and could say that I tried to help in good faith with everything I had.

Well, if any of you face technology issues on a regular basis, you will understand what it means to look at your computer and to want to chuck it out of the window. As with learning any new software programs or online systems, there is a certain level of "frustration" that comes along with the process. For those of us who like to know what we are doing and like to feel confident in our actions, learning something new can be a challenge to that part of the ego. About the 50th time you try to get something technical to work or if things are dependent on the time lines of two support teams with whom you only work remotely, things can be very tight around deadlines and bring up emotions that cause you to lose patience or, plainly, your ever loving mind.

There were times when I looked at myself in the mirror and asked myself if I could actually do it, and do it well. Trying to accomplish something new of this magnitude with no training and a full life that also requires my attention at the same time was difficult. I have a family, friends, and a full-time job, not to mention the fact that I made commitments to myself spiritually and physically to do certain practices for my personal wellbeing. Could I cram it all in? Sometimes, it didn't feel possible. When I was sleep deprived as I faced a deadline or was facing a wall of immense technological proportions, it sometimes felt like too much. And, when we are pulled and stressed to our gills, the ego loves to chime in right at that moment: "Give up! Give in! Give over! Call Swamiji and cry uncle! You did everything you could. It is just too much. You are tired. You tried. No shame in not being able to do something! Throw that computer out the window!"

However, fortunately, I know the value of a breath…several breaths…those deep breaths down into the Self that fill your person and stifle that ego. I took a minute and breathed. I also remembered that I could ask for help, beseech Consciousness for the gifts of grace, fortitude, perspective and laughter. I also remembered my mantra work, saying it on repeat as I went back to work. With these tools from Sacred Feet Yoga, I could kick the ego in the can and go back at it reenergized and with a positive attitude.

By employing those tools, with the help of the divine, I was able to make books. It is as simple as that. It was something I'd never done or imagined doing or had training to do, and I was able to push past "limitations" to grow and learn and make something.

As a wise Guru once said, seva takes away the blocks on the spiritual path and supports you to achieve your goals. She says that you perform seva and you are sure to change as you experience greater purpose in life and an intimate relationship of the Self. With true selfless service, you become one with Consciousness and receive the benefits of that bliss.

Of course, there are many forms of seva. It is different for everyone. However, that wise Guru whose ashram is located in upstate New York says that what matters in offering seva is: the attitude with which you offer your service, the intention behind your service, your expectation of reward, your willingness to offer your service, and the way you perform your seva.

As we break out into groups, I would like you to think about two things:

First, what is your seva? How do you offer seva? Do you know? If you have not thought about exactly what you offer in selfless service, I invite you to do so now.

Second, how are you offering your seva? Are you aware of the attitude with which you approach it? Are you mindfully offering your actions? Are you holding back? Do you have attachment to your efforts or perhaps have some emotions coming up for you as you offer it? Are you doing it because you should but your heart isn't really in it? Are you looking at your seva as connecting with the divine to become love or the divine-in-action, operating from the highest matrika? Let's discuss.

Ok, I am incredibly enthusiastic to hear about your seva. Would any of you like to share your thoughts that came up in the group discussions? Who would like to start us off?

Meditation for Offering Seva

Sit in a chair or on a cushion on the floor with your spine straight, shoulders back, head resting lightly on your neck, palms gently placed face down on your thighs, and fingers straight or in chin mudra. Relax your face. Start to notice your breath as it flows in and out of your body. Breathe in deeply. Breathe out long.

As you breathe in deeply, and as you breathe out long, in the context of offering seva or yourselves selflessly, let The Fourth Teachings of Sacred Feet Yoga ride the breath, taking you into your deepest Self and aligning you with the highest good of the divine. Repeat them to yourself as you breathe in and out, settling into the meditation.

Live your life peacefully—and with purpose.
Maintain a glad sense of humor.
Place your faith in stillness, steadiness, and service.

As the teachings are breathed in and out of your bodies, feel them reinforce the virtues and positive ways of being that are ever present within your Selves. Feel your hearts resonate with peace, purpose, a glad sense of humor, stillness, and steadiness. As you breathe, feel the vibration of the sacred within and the intimacy of being connected to the divine in this goodness. Open your heart of hearts and beseech the divine to radiate goodness outward from your Self to fill all of you—your thoughts, your speech, and your physical actions.

Feel the goodness radiating out from within, the sacred light and heat extending to the tip of your toes and the crown of your head. Feel the freedom as the divine light and heat fill every cell of your body. With every in-breath and out-breath, you are one with divine goodness.

When you feel ready, slowly prepare to come back to the room. You will open your eyes to the outer world but the inner connection forged through the heart in this meditation with the divine will not close. With a ready, open heart, be of service, however that may manifest.

Namaste.

III. Simplicity, Selfless Service, Prophecy

Element 7: Simplicity of Life and Lifestyle

Element 8: Compassionate Service

Element 9: Prophetic Voice and Action

The Interspiritual Paradigm—
Legacies and Horizons

Dr. Kurt Johnson

On April 29-May 1, 2016 members of the Community of The Mystic Heart (officially organized in January 2010) held their first international residential retreat. I was asked to share about the history and legacy of CMH as well as join Sw. Shraddhananda and Mirabai Starr in reflections on Br. Wayne Teasdale's Nine Elements of a Universal Spirituality. I was particularly asked to center on elements 7-9: (7) Living a life of simplicity; (8) Being of selfless service and compassionate action; and (9) Empowering the prophetic voice for justice, compassion, and world transformation.

Legacies

Worldwide, the Interspiritual phenomenon now enters a second decade of development since the life—as "a monk in the world"—of Br. Wayne Teasdale who coined the term in his now classic book, *The Mystic Heart: Discovering a Universal Spirituality in the World's Religions*, in 1999.[1] Following from that initial usage, as of this writing there are about 100,000 entries under "Interspirituality" at Google and similar Internet search engines. If Interspirituality is simply seen as what religions and spirituality do as the world globalizes and goes multi-cultural, then the Interspiritual paradigm was a destined aspect of our ongoing human evolution.

As a result, there is a profound historical process currently unfolding—the rapid manifestation of a globally emergent "universal spirituality" inherently connected to the compelling moral and ethical values underpinning the world's Great Wisdom Traditions. The difference today is that the shared deep moral and ethical values *themselves* are now being emphasized, gradually eclipsing particular religious creeds and dogmas which (in the more superficial dimension of ideas or beliefs) previously characterized a more fractured and parochial landscape among the world's religions.

It is important that people understand what has happened. And, as scholars of this process, it's important that we narrow down, and record, our understandings of factors that have contributed to this meteoric growth of the Interspiritual paradigm. A major background to this development (known by some but not by all) was the thirty-some year process of the Snowmass Interreligious Initiative continued by Father Thomas Keating, and others, after its origination by His Holiness the Dalai Lama, Ken Wilber, and numerous other pioneer Interfaith luminaries. It involved delegates from across all the world's traditions, creating the "Nine Points of Agreement" among the world's religions."

Further, from these then emerged a distinct values and ethical component regarding the new universal spirituality articulated as the "Nine Elements of a Universal Spirituality" by Br. Wayne [MH: 109-157]. Globally now, most Interfaith discussions are based, knowingly or unknowingly, on these elements or principles.

The Nine Points of Agreement put forward by the Snowmass Initiative include these shared principles:

1. The world religions bear witness to the experience of Ultimate Reality to which they give various names:

Brahma, Allah, (the) Absolute, God, Great Spirit.
2. Ultimate Reality cannot be limited by any name or concept.
3. Ultimate Reality is the ground of infinite potentiality and actualization.
4. Faith is opening, accepting, and responding to Ultimate Reality. Faith in this sense precedes every belief system.
5. The potential for human wholeness—or in other frames of reference, enlightenment, salvation, transformation, blessedness, nirvana—is present in every human.
6. Ultimate Reality may be experienced not only through religious practices but also through nature, art, human relationships, and service to others.
7. As long as the human condition is experienced as separate from Ultimate Reality, it remains subject to ignorance, illusion, weakness, and suffering.
8. Disciplined practice is essential to the spiritual life; yet spiritual attainment isn't the result of one's own efforts, but the result of the experience of oneness (unity) with Ultimate Reality.
9. Prayer is communion with Ultimate Reality, whether it's regarded as personal, impersonal (transpersonal), or beyond both.

These are the more mental, intellectual, or "left-brain" elements of the consensus that has been arising across the world's religions for the last three decades.

On the other hand, the "Nine Elements of a Universal Spirituality" reflect the traits of personal character, or spiritual maturity, that would reflect the values inherent in the Nine Points of Agreement. The Nine Elements not only represent the aspirations of authentic spirituality but also describe its goals and fruits. Each circumscribes a realm of spiritual and ethical inquiry and responsibility, and each contains multiple aspects that are critical to global Interfaith harmony education. They were the central points of discussion among the recent retreatants of CMH:

1. Actualizing full moral and ethical capacity
2. Living in harmony with the cosmos and all living beings
3. Cultivating a life of deep nonviolence
4. Living in humility and gratitude
5. Embracing a regular spiritual practice
6. Cultivating mature self-knowledge
7. Living a life of simplicity
8. Being of selfless service and compassionate action
9. Empowering the prophetic voice for justice, compassion, and world transformation

As of 2013, when Kurt Johnson and David Robert Ord published *The Coming Interspiritual Age*[iii], a combination of the above principles, added to three other lists of Interfaith consensus points drawn from the work of Br. Wayne Teasdale, became known as "The Interspiritual Declaration"[iv] and, as such, has been mentioned in United Nations and other international documents and venues as one of a number of internationally vetted consensus points of an Interfaith spirituality.[v] In sum, these principles— springing from whatever language is used (Brahma, Allah, the Absolute, God, Great Spirit etc.)—emphasize the great ethical and wisdom teachings of the religions, with their stress on the grandeur of humanity—a grandeur that is not only the heart of authentic religion but of the arts, including literature, poetry, music, art, dance, and all the other manifestations that mark *Homo sapiens* as an unparalleled species.

It is not by accident that these unifying ethical principles represent one of the aspects of inherent religious unity that was realized by fruitful discussion across the world religions after the pivotal 2nd Vatican Council ("Vatican II" 1962-65). Global discussions following Vatican II (often called "the Foundationalist Discussions") [TCIA: 244-247] defined three potential unifying or "Archimedean" principles possible among all the world's religions. These include:

1. Their common mystical core—experiential "unity consciousness"
2. Universal ethical teachings and behavior aspirations
3. Mutual commitment to the self-evident truths of economic and social justice.

In the West, participants in these post Vatican II conversations included such historical luminaries as Thomas Merton, Wilfred Cantwell Smith, Harvey Cox, John Cobb, Langdon Gilkey, Juan Luis Segundo, Karl Rahner, Jeremy Bernstein, Raimon Panikkar, and Hans Küng. Of these, Merton and Pannikar are also universally identified with the emergence of the Interspiritual paradigm, because when the Foundationalist Discussion was later opposed by subsequent Vatican encyclicals, Merton and Panikkar continued to insist on the historical veracity of the first Archimedean unifying principle listed above. Harvey Cox joined in this rebellion against subsequent Vatican authority based on the third Archimedean principle, consistent with the then popular views of Liberation Theology (also later widely opposed by then Vatican authorities).

Ultimately, the potential of each of these principals

in manifesting actual unity remains a question. This question vexed the early explorers of this conversation. Generally, when the Roman Catholicism of the time turned against the Foundationalist Discussion, the more conventional theologians, those more bound by conventional creed or belief, concluded that unity points might actually not be possible and bowed to ecclesiastical authority. However, as noted, the mystics and liberation theologians among them—Thomas Merton and Raimon Pannikar, together with the liberation thinker Harvey Cox—took the *experiential* position that the shared existential/mystical core of all the world's traditions was *synonymous* with true commitment to building a world based on the shared values of all the traditions. Shared values and ethics of love, kindness, selfless service and equanimity are central to the teachings of all the Great Traditions. Further, they have been principal to the historical reform and revival movements that have characterized all the traditions as well, and those that arose with the advent of modern secular and religious Humanism.

When forgotten by the traditions themselves, or made subservient by political or financial pathology, these same values sprang up in independent movements. Humanism is, perhaps, the best example—the legacy of Ethical Culture in America or Auguste Comte in Europe, among other humanist movements—which declared that this shared ethos was, in fact, the core of religious experience itself: deed over creed. And, these values have become the hallmark of the currently emerging global Interspiritual Movement.

From Einstein to Schweitzer, King to Mandela, the number of social heroes who have embraced and emanated from such movements is huge. Indeed, this sense of shared ethos spawned all the great movements across the globe in the turbulent times of social and political change that typified what is generally called the Integrative Age unfolding since the 1970s. The unifying principle generally acknowledged as the fourth Archimedean point of the world's religions—the shared commitment to social and economic justice—is rooted in this emerging Integrative Era as well [TCIA: 373-378].

The Interspiritual Movement

This Integrative Era, now moving toward a new Holistic Era, a powerful underpinning from the global Interfaith Movement, has moved rapidly to a maturing Interspiritual Movement. Of this, Br. Wayne Teasdale (who named the "Interspiritual" movement as the direction that religion must go to accommodate the needs of authentic globalization and multiculturalism) said, in his now classic book *The Mystic Heart: Discovering a Universal Spirituality in the World's Religions:*

> "This revolution will be the task of the Interspiritual Age. The necessary shifts in consciousness require a new approach to spirituality that transcends past religious cultures of fragmentation and isolation. We need to understand, to really grasp at an elemental level that the definitive revolution is the spiritual awakening of humankind." [MH: 4]

In retrospect, it can be said that the modern-day "Interspiritual Movement" begins, implicitly, with the appearance of Br. Wayne's books (*The Mystic Heart, A Monk in the World,* and *Bede Griffiths, an Introduction to his Interspiritual*

Thought) prior to his untimely passing in 2004. However, it inevitably has "morphed" in a manner to be "owned by everyone" as much of the Interfaith world inevitably moved from an Interfaith understanding to an Interspiritual understanding—in effect "from head to heart" over the next decades. Today, Interspirituality is virtually synonymous with movements and narratives as wide ranging as "spiritual but not religious," "unaffiliated," "nones," "universal-, global-, or worldcentric-spirituality," "multiple belonging," "evolutionary spirituality," and many, many more. And today, large numbers of previously conventional academic and seminary institutions have broadly defined Interfaith and Interspiritual programs and curricula. Many of these are sometimes not even aware of the history above, which incubated modern Interspirituality from the original Foundationalist Discussion and the pioneering work of those like Merton, Teasdale, Griffths, Panikkar and Keating.

The Interspiritual Movement as it is centered around "The Interspiritual Network"[vi] has been, for at least the first decade after Br. Wayne's passing (until it inevitably went global as everyone discovered it), *the* or *one of the* incipient hubs of the paradigm.

Short History of The Interspiritual Movement

In 2001, Br. Wayne referred to the fledgling group of "Interspirituals" around him as "the association." It was formalized as a New York not for profit corporation (Interspiritual Dialogue Inc.) in 2002, in *ad hoc* association with the United Nations NGO community in what was then the "Spiritual Caucus" of the UN NGO community, before the modern-day era of officially credentialed UN

NGO "Committees" existed. Interspiritual Dialogue conducted numerous activities, including a major presentation on Interspirituality at the Parliament of the World's Religions in Barcelona in 2004.[vii] Following Br. Wayne's passing in 2004, and a tribute event for him in 2005, the Interspirituals created a major web presence which then rapidly expanded to become the web resource website "The Interspiritual Multiplex,"[viii] which continues to exist to this day, albeit in an old web format. One can fast forward then to "The Dawn of Interspirituality Conference" in 2013, which took place shortly after the issue of my book *The Coming Interspiritual Age* and joined over 100 organizations worldwide promulgating the Interspiritual paradigm.[ix] It formed a committee to build a new modernized website, now The Interspiritual Network at www.interspirituality.com.

Elements of the network then joined in influential ways with the Eco-Spiritual Movement anchored in the vision of seminal eco-theologian Fr. Thomas Berry, creating affiliate organizations known today as "Self Care to Earth Care"[x] and its United Nations collegial organization known as Forum 21 Institute.[xi] These entities, respectively more ecological and sociological in nature, further promulgated the Interspiritual message in arenas of activism. By 2016, this had further culminated in the partnerships with other global Interfaith and Interspiritual networks (i.e. Australian and Asian entities 1God.com, WorldWeavers.com, Unity.earth and UDAY.com) to create "The Convergence" radio series with VoiceAmerica[xii] and the emerging international web education platform "The Convergence Academy."[xiii]

Short History of the Community of The Mystic Heart

Br. Wayne Teasdale, in all three of his previously cited books, envisioned a "Universal Order of Sannyasa," an international Interfaith organization in which persons could translate the traditional "Sannyas" vows of monastic commitment and a life of service to transformative work to a multi-faith global perspective. Wayne himself had emulated this role, as recorded in his book *A Monk in the World*, by wearing the saffron ("kavi") robes of the traditional Hindu "Sannyas" and serving in a lifestyle fashioned after the Hindu-Christian Sannyas of Bede Griffiths' original Sannyas community at Shantivanam in India. In 2003 Francis Cardinal George sanctioned Br. Wayne's vows in this life of service and appointed him as "Official Hermit" of the Diocese of Chicago.

Of his Universal Order of Sannyasa vision Br. Wayne said:

"Perhaps one day we will witness the eventual emergence of a universal order of sannyas: contemplative or mystics from all traditions united in their awareness, their love, and their dedication to earth and humankind, and all sentient beings. As mystics in the world are we not creating this universal order? Are we not allies of the natural world in its struggle to be and to see harmony with the human? Do we not thereby become natural advocates for the homeless, the poor, the marginalized, the oppressed, the starving, the diseased? This universal order has the pressing task of raising the consciousness of the world, to that highest level…to which all the great spiritual paths are dedicated" [MH: 201].

In his Interspiritual thought, Br. Wayne consistently uses the word "Sannyasa" to have universal connotations.

The Universal Order of Sannyasa was envisioned by Br. Wayne, in each of these now classic books, as a modern gathering of those committed to a life dedicated to deep spiritual practice, sacred service or activism, and advancement of the Interspiritual message…that life in the heart knows no boundaries in creed or belief but is a modern gathering of persons from many and varied life circumstances, dedicated to a lifestyle possible and appropriate for them within this deep intention [MH: 16].

Further, Teasdale continued to say: "The term sannyasa, referring to renunciation, points to all those saints, seers, sages, ascetics, and yogis, over thousands of years who have renounced the world and made possible something beyond the comprehension of religion, something that transcends religion, because it is infinite and ineffable. It eludes the capacity of any concept or doctrine to express or contain it" [MH: 248, in part].

And, of the makeup of such a Universal Order of Sannyasa, he said:

"It should be an Interspiritual order…open to all people—men and women, married and single, young, middle-aged, and old, confused or clear, adherents or not, with faith or agnostic—united in their desire for a deeper, more meaningful life. This would be a truly universal society of sannyasa, an order that welcomes as members individuals from all the world's religions and even from no tradition at all"[MH: 248, in part].

It is generally appreciated today that it was highly unlikely that Br. Wayne's rather "monolithic" view of what could emerge in an international consensus as a "Universal Order of Sannyasa" could actually materialize. In retrospect, this is because of (1) the diversity of interpretations that "Sannyas" had across numerous traditions; (2) the fact that the Interspiritual movement grew and diversified so fast it negated the potential role of any individual seminal organization as a success "center" for such an enterprise; and (3) because Br. Wayne did not anticipate the demographic effects of history's now massive trend toward global "religious disaffiliation" which has negatively affected the number of persons in religious orders across all traditions worldwide.

Br. Wayne was a person of what Ken Wilber calls "Second Tier Consciousness." It was easy for him to comprehend a boundary-less concept of multi-faith Sannyasa in service to the world. However, as Wilber notes in *Integral Spirituality*, most (especially committed) religious adherents have a "First Tier View" where the allegiance still goes to their group, their creed, and their "way." Ultimately, Br. Wayne's view of sannyas organizations melding across traditions on a global level depended, in part, on their ongoing existence as primary and thriving organizations in their own right. In today's environment of widespread religious disaffiliation, this is simply no longer the demographic reality internationally.

Accordingly, what was founded in 2010 as The Universal Order of Sannyasa, in line with the vision in Br. Wayne's books, modified its name to the Community of The Mystic Heart (CMH) soon after. As the current website states: "Although the Universal Order of Sannyas was the name used by Br. Wayne Teasdale throughout his writing, we found that use of term 'Sannyas' in a non-traditional sense caused discomfort for some traditional Sannyasins and, further, the term was unfamiliar, or seemed too exclusive, to others in the unfolding international Interspiritual dialogue."

Accordingly, it can be said that, today, CMH is one

of the many "experiments" (TCIA: 346-361) going on worldwide with Interspiritual experience and Interspiritual living. CMH itself, as of the residential retreat, the occasion of this volume, is itself changing and continues to experiment with new ideas as to how monastic Interspirituality can be lived out. Since the retreat, and largely organized there, CMH is providing at least two tracks for how individuals might live out the vision of Br. Wayne in *The Mystic Heart* and *A Monk in the World*. One is a more "traditional" full Sannyas component shepherded by Swami Shraddhananda and headquartered at Slate Branch Ashram.[xiv] The other is the new "Interspiritual Monastics in the World" initiative which nurtures a broad, and highly individually defined, life of spiritual practice and sacred activism with which CMH members can experiment.[xv] ISMW has been taking shape over the last months and can be examined further, as noted above, at the Community of The Mystic Heart website.

Horizons

It appears inevitable now, with "spiritual but not religious," "unaffiliated," "nones," "universal-, global-, or worldcentric-spirituality," "multiple belonging," "evolutionary spirituality," and many more descriptive names pervasive worldwide today, that "Interspirituality" is now "owned" and empowered by multiple interpretations. This very likely reflects a natural evolution from the incipient predictions of Br. Wayne Teasdale about religions and spirituality in a world rapidly going global and multi-cultural. Indeed, it appears we have already transitioned from the seminal era in which pioneers like Teasdale pointed out this inevitable evolutionary trend and are now seeing the manifestation of a diversity of ways worldwide that this globalization of religion and spirituality is happening. Thus, in many ways at this point, we can say that this is a "happy ending" to a process just beginning. However, we cannot ignore the plethora of ways that religions and spirituality are still acting from worldviews at far lower levels of development characterized, regularly and at their worst, by all the cruel and heinous things that people and groups do to others "in the name of their loving God." Obviously it is not enough to have somewhere under 20%, or even a firm 10%, of the world (to use statistics from Ken Wilber[xvi]) living out their religion and spirituality in a climate of truly unconditional love and caring. But this is still the hope and the inevitable direction—that the world's religions will continue to move their praxis to higher and higher levels of behavioral development.

This predicament re-echoes the implications of the last three elements of the Nine Elements of a Universal Spirituality I was asked to address at this retreat. Certainly, the ultimate expression of "simplicity" is Br. Wayne's statement that the only viable religion for the third millennium would be spirituality itself [MH: 26]. And assuredly, all the experiments with Interspirituality and Interspiritual community have been an examination and pursuit of that vision. Being of selfless service and compassionate action follows in tow. The tens, if not hundreds, of leader-level individuals who have contributed to the growth and expansion of Interspirituality (see the speaker profiles at the 2013 Dawn of Interspirituality Conference[xvii] as well as the biographical profiles in *Mature Interspirituality*) exemplify that reality. Empowering the prophetic voice for justice, compassion, and world transformation has "been their business" and will continue to be germane in the ongoing process of how religions and spirituality "go global" and become the universal spirituality of our planet's future.

As one incipient part of this process, the recording of all this on the historic occasion of the first residential retreat of the 2016 Community of The Mystic Heart has certainly been useful, not only to each of us personally but to the ongoing process of the unfolding of an inevitably Interspiritual world civilization.

---

[i] Teasdale, Wayne. 1999. *The Mystic Heart: Discovering a Universal Spirituality in the World's Religions.* Novato CA: New World Library [hereafter "MH" for citation of specific page numbers].

[ii] Miles-Yepez, Netanel [Ed.]. 2006. *The Common Heart: An Experience of Interreligious Dialogue.* Brooklyn NY: Lantern Books, as adapted and updated by Johnson, Kurt and David Robert Ord. 2013. *The Coming Interspiritual Age.* Vancouver CN: Namaste Publishing p 341 [hereafter "TCIA" for citation of specific page numbers].

[iii] Johnson, Kurt and David Robert Ord. 2013. *The Coming Interspiritual Age.* Vancouver CN: Namaste Publishing

[iv] http://www.thecominginterspiritualage.com/initiatives#The-Interspiritual-Declaration

[v] http://www.forum21.co/at-the-united-nations

[vi] www.interspirituality.com

[vii] http://www.kosmosjournal.org/article/tension-in-barcelonaparliament-of-worlds-religions-2004/

[viii] www.isdna.org **and** http://multiplex.isdna.org/

[ix] http://www.satyana.org/dawn_interspirituality_2013.html

[x] www.selfcaretoearthcare.com

[xi] www.forum21.co

[xii] https://www.voiceamerica.com/show/2610/the-convergence

[xiii] http://1god.academy/

[xiv] http://communityofthemysticheart.org/monastic-options

[xv] http://communityofthemysticheart.org/monastic-options

[xvi] https://www.youtube.com/watch?v=114jcxxl_0ok; https://www.integrallife.com/video/revolutionary-spirituality

[xvii] http://www.satyana-conferences.org/

'Speak Me Into Silence:'
How the Practice of Silence Has Inspired and Shaped My Interspiritual Journey

Lynda "Ma Shanti" Terry

"Solitude is the teacher and silence is the teaching."
—Br. Wayne Teasdale

Silence has been the most valuable and instructive of the spiritual practices that have been part of my Interspiritual journey. In fact, I have come to view silence as the practice that is most inherently Interspiritual in nature— meaning, that it provides the most universal container for mystical experience, as well as serves as the most universal language that can be spoken between a mystic of any tradition and the Ineffable One she or he seeks to know. Certainly this has been true for me. Silence has been and continues to be the primary catalyst for my own process of Interspiritual maturation.

My practice of silence has included many intentional forms, such as choosing to take part in a 10-day silent meditation retreat or joining others in a moment of silence during a worship service or silently "holding space" for a collective purpose or situation (as I did for the Nine Elements retreat in Kentucky, when I was unable to attend due to illness). But my most dramatic and instructive experiences of silence have been those of the capital S category, when Silence has chosen me.

Silence has a penchant for seeking out and seducing the mystically inclined, which is how it was for me—a gradual, but inevitable seduction. It began simply enough—

the unexpected gift of a few seconds of quiet mind in my very first meditation experience. Now, more than 25 years since that first taste, Silence weaves through everything I think, feel, say and do. I'm never unaware of its presence, and this relationship with Silence has been essential in bringing me to the Interspiritual path—in fact, I think of it as a "divine conspiracy" perpetrated between the two (with many willing accomplices also helping along the way).

When I first touched into those few seconds of silence in my early forties, during a meditation class I took to help me cope with some stressful life events, it was so profound, even though brief, that I resolved then and there, to meditate daily for the rest of my life. Over time, the periods of inner quiet grew longer and led to many positive changes, inner and outer—including improvements in my health, career and relationships as well as the opportunity to teach others to meditate. But after a few years, I began to feel a call to find a more consciously spiritual context to what I was experiencing and teaching. This longing led me, over the course of a decade, to a Hindu spiritual teacher at an ashram in upstate New York, to the silent meditation group of a Sufi spiritual teacher on the Northern California coast, and to a Catholic-affiliated hermitage in the hills overlooking Sonoma Valley, California.

These three places and the traditions— Hinduism/Yoga, Naqshbandi Sufism and Catholic Christianity—that they represent have served as cauldrons for my evolution from spiritual seeker to Interspiritual mystic. In every case, the single most potent ingredient in the spiritual stew they offer me is Silence.

You might wonder, where along the way does Interspirituality enter the picture? Outwardly, it was via *The Mystic Heart*, which I first read in 1999. But inwardly, the

Interspiritual path came for me via a recurring dream that I began to have in 1998—a year before Teasdale's book was published.

In this dream, I am seated on the floor of a small room or hut, which is illuminated by candlelight, and across from me, sits an older man with white hair, white beard and intensely blue eyes. He wears a simple orange-colored robe-like garment. This man never speaks to me in the dream; he simply looks at me in a loving yet compelling way with those amazing eyes. I also do not speak in the dream; I just keep returning his gaze. We are completely silent together, and we are completely held in that state by the Silence.

Every time I awoke from this dream, I felt as if something important had occurred, but could not get a clear sense of what that meant and could not place the man as anyone I knew in my waking life. The dream did remind me, though, of a verse from a favorite poem, "Mystical Discourse," written by my dear friend, the scholar and author Dr. Sonya Jones, now known as Sw. Shraddhananda. In the poem, she writes:

> *How does one*
> *say silence*
> *fluid as it falls*
> *between us*
> *bodies floating*
> *like steel feathers*
> *invisible sinews*
> *of trust?*

The poem describes a meeting with her Hindu guru, where no one else was present, and no words were outwardly spoken. They simply sit together, "speaking," in silence the entire time.

By the time I began having my recurring dream, I too was a student of this same guru (thanks to my friend's introduction to her), but this holy woman was more my age, not an old man with white hair. Who was the mysterious, kindly elder of my dreams? Was another teacher meant to come into my life? Why did the silent communion we shared in the dream feel so profound, so important?

When I discovered *The Mystic Heart* in a metaphysical bookstore that was located near the ashram of my guru, it actually was the sub-title, "Discovering a Universal Spirituality in the World's Religions," that inspired me to purchase the book. I had become rather obsessed by then, in learning more about the meditation practices of different spiritual paths, as well as with the idea of being able to honor, appreciate and even practice more than one tradition. I was raised a Protestant Christian, but as a very young girl, also had been exposed to Roman Catholic ritual—and a deep pull to Catholicism periodically would re-surface throughout my life. My meditation practice and teaching had inspired me to learn more about Eastern traditions as well, and a strong resonance with Yoga philosophy eventually led me to find and commit to the Hindu teacher of my friend's poems.

I was fascinated and inspired by the fact that my teacher's talks, books, videos and other offerings frequently featured quotes, stories, music, etc. from traditions other than Yoga—and she especially liked to share stories and wisdom of the many great mystics. Her approach gave me permission, in essence, to indulge my intuitive preference for a multi-tradition foundation to my spiritual life. So, seeing the sub-title of Teasdale's book sent a surge of excitement through me; I had to learn more about this concept of Universal Spirituality.

The Mystic Heart and its offering of Interspirituality as a potential path rocked my inner world. I was hungry to know more, and began searching for additional information about people and ideas mentioned in the book—which led me to look online for more about Teasdale's mentor, Fr. Bede Griffiths. When I found a website about Fr. Bede's work that included photographs of him, I was stunned. The man in my recurring dream was Fr. Bede!

At that moment, I understood the dream to have been a form of mystical initiation…like a darshan or blessing welcoming me onto the Interspiritual path. I also understood that it was most significant that this blessing was conveyed in and through Silence.

Over the next couple of years, I happily expanded my spiritual life and learning to include the Interspiritual approach that Br. Wayne shared in *The Mystic Heart*. I read everything I could find about and by Fr. Bede and others who were seen as pioneers in the field. I continued my daily meditation practice and teaching of meditation. I also continued to visit my Hindu teacher's ashram to study, practice and offer seva, or selfless service. I was happy, fulfilled, blossoming spiritually…and then, almost overnight, my practice of Silence dramatically changed.

In early 2001, I began to experience such a compelling longing for Silence that it became an obsession. It surfaced first—and quite appropriately—in my daily meditation practice, as I began sitting more than once a day and for longer periods. Soon it also became a persistent subtext in other areas of my life, such as preferring quiet as the backdrop to my daily tasks. My longing was not just for physical quiet, though, but also, for the deepening of my inner silence; I yearned to dive into the great ocean of supreme Silence that my teacher spoke of as the higher Self …the Absolute…God.

In April 2001, I went to see a woman visionary I had heard about from friends. I did not go for any particular reason—just a feeling that it was something I was to do. Very early in the session she named my longing and offered these startling and quite specific comments about it:

> *"The path of silence is your service in this life—part of your gift to this planet…Silence and meditation is how you serve best—it's one of the ways you are helping to coach the planet through change…[helping] to still the trembling of the mind called fear. For the problem of the planet is the disturbance of minds, and what can still the disturbance except silence?"*

Humbled and inspired by her message, I began reading anything I could find that dealt with silence as a more intentional act and as a primary spiritual practice—especially in the context of service to others. I signed up for a weeklong retreat at my spiritual teacher's ashram, the format of which would encourage being silent and inward, and I made plans for my first 10-day solo silent retreat that December, when I would have the house to myself while my husband was away on a trip. These lines from Swami Shraddhananda's poem held particular resonance for me during this time:

> *We can't say silence well*
> *silence speaks itself*
> *it speaks us.*

In June, at the weeklong meditation retreat, I maintained silence as much as possible. It was my first time staying at the ashram for that long a period and my first "deep dive" into maintaining outer silence for long stretches of time over a period of days.

Ironically, there were many episodes, during that retreat, when the environment around me was anything but silent. Loud traffic noise near the temple, someone coughing repeatedly during the meditations, talkative roommates in the dorm room where I was staying. Yet, through it all, Silence was making its presence known to me…speaking itself. I felt as if I were being "trained" in how to let Silence "speak me," as my Swami friend's poem says—how to consistently hold awareness of an inner stillness despite what my senses were experiencing.

It was difficult for me to return home from the retreat at the ashram and resume my prior daily schedule. I wasn't ready to let my "conversation" with Silence go. So I decided to commit to being in silence every evening from 10 p.m. through breakfast the next day, a commitment my husband was willing to honor, as long as I didn't expect him to be silent too!

This approach seemed to sate my hunger for silence for a time, but by summer's end, a surprising shift in my meditation practice signaled yet another "training" for me to undergo. It began a couple of days before the September 11th terrorist attacks. Instead of meditating at my usual practice time every morning, I started being drawn into meditation spontaneously, at different times of the day. I could be in the kitchen preparing lunch, and would get a silent inward "command" to go to my meditation seat, and fall spontaneously into deep meditative silence—sometimes for hours.

After the September 11th attacks occurred, this pattern not only continued, but I also was guided to change where I sat for meditation, so that I could face in a different direction. I felt no resentment or even curiosity about the change; I was completely surrendered to this inner prompting that had no words to it…just a knowing to go sit and be in silence.

Eventually, I became aware of a connection between the timing of these inner calls to silence, and events occurring in my environment in the immediate aftermath of 9/11.

Our home at the time was located in southern Pennsylvania, close to the Maryland border. Catoctin Mountain—the location of Camp David, the mountain retreat for the President of the United States—was just a few miles south of our home. In fact, one could see the very mountain range where Camp David was situated from our living room windows and sunroom.

In those first few days after the attacks, Camp David was the secure location where President Bush and his team were reported to be staying while they dealt with the crisis. The sound of US Air Force fighter jets flying overhead several times a day were the giveaway that the President and his team were at the mountain retreat. And for a time, in those early days, I was being inwardly directed to go meditate whenever those jets flew over our house.

As it turned out, the new direction of my meditation seat situated me so I was directly facing that mountain range. When I made this connection, I was shocked. A coincidence? Or was my silent meditation energy being "called up" for service in some way? I will never know. I only know that, when the jets flew over our house, I was compelled to follow the silent inner direction to do what I did. It felt right, and it felt important, so I simply trusted.

As was true for so many Americans, my life changed

after 9/11. In my case, the tragedy was the first experience where I connected my personal spiritual practice with a larger purpose, with being of service through meditation, with surrendering my mind's ideas to a deeper, heart-centered wisdom that arose from the silence and stillness of my practice.

In October 2001, I read a book, *The Third Coming*, written by Unity Church minister, Jim Rosemergy, which seemed to confirm the importance of silence as a practice that could transform not just individuals, but, perhaps, the world. In this book, he spoke of a time when larger and larger masses of people would feel drawn to gather in silence—perhaps in a time of global crisis—and how this response would create a beneficial shift in human consciousness. What I read inspired me to apply for an extended residency at my teacher's ashram, to begin in spring 2002. It would be easier to spend more time in silence and meditation there, with other silence-loving kindred spirits, and I also could offer seva—selfless service—to my teacher while in residence. My husband applied also, and in November 2001, we got word that our application was approved.

I committed to spend the 10 days before Christmas in solo retreat, in our home, while my husband was away on his trip. It would be the first time I had ever spent that many consecutive days in silence and by myself, rather than with a group, but I was eager for the opportunity. I felt I was being asked to do this…to prepare for something that was coming. I couldn't grasp what it was, only that the retreat would ready me for it.

I must admit that staying silent and in solitude for those 10 days was one of the hardest things I have ever done. But it also was a revelation—and the insights, ideas, and experiences from those 10 days continue to bear fruit in my life nearly two decades later.

The most compelling and significant development to come out of my solo retreat was a strong premonition that my Hindu teacher's annual New Year's Day message, to be revealed in an audio teleconference program on January 1, 2002, would have something to do with silence. Though the announcement of an annual theme of study and practice for the year had been a tradition of our teacher for several years, and Satellite Intensives had been offered, this was the first time in the history of the New Year's message that a live broadcast of this nature had ever been offered.

Each year, the new theme was very effectively kept a secret until the moment our teacher spoke it, so there had been no rumors or "leaks" as to what it might be. But I just kept getting this inner sense that it would somehow relate to my overwhelming obsession with silence. There was no logic to this; among the tens of thousands of followers of my teacher around the world, it was pretty unlikely that my particular experiences and longings would somehow be acknowledged through this annual tradition. But there was no logic about my obsession with silence either. I was like the subject of a Rumi poem—besotted with Silence, mad with devotion to it—helplessly and happily so.

On January 1, 2002, I was alone at home, as my husband's return would not be for another few weeks. At the appointed time, I called in to join the teleconference and waited through the preliminary ceremonies for the moment my teacher would share the theme for our yogic study and practice in the year ahead. After greeting us warmly and leading us in a chanted invocation, she began to speak. Within minutes, my intuition was confirmed: silence was the focus for 2002!

With this dramatic moment of confirmation from my teacher, everything that I thought I knew about who I was and where I was going in my life and spiritual journey, changed. It was a kind of near-death experience, and intensely emotional, as events of the 12 years since I began to meditate flashed through my mind…the instant affinity for meditation…the intense response to silence and stillness…the shift towards a multi-tradition spiritual philosophy and practice…the discovery of Interspirituality via *The Mystic Heart*…the profound experience of the dream darshans with Fr. Bede…the dramatic changes in my meditation and silence practices following 9/11…the strong guidance to apply for extended residency at my teacher's ashram in 2002, the year when the entire focus of our path's world community would be on the very practice with which I had become obsessed.

All of the above had led me to an interweaving of the practice of silence with the insights and changes brought about through walking an Interspiritual path. That interweaving continues to this day and, I expect, will continue until my last breath.

"The paths are many," Br. Wayne Teasdale wrote in *The Mystic Heart* (79), "but the goal is the same: discovering the way."

Further, as Br. Wayne notes, "Letting go and letting be are…the fruit of years of spiritual practice through the day-to-day labor of meditation. Attaining inner quiet, seeking stillness of mind and senses, requires enormous discipline…"

He continues: "*The Maitri Upanishad* expresses this with great beauty, accuracy, and paradox: 'There is something beyond our mind which abides in silence within our mind. It is the supreme mystery beyond thought. Let one's mind and subtle body rest upon that and not rest on anything else.' To rest beyond our mind and yet to be present in silence within the mind, means that the divine cannot be grasped by the mind's methods through reason. The divine is ineffable because infinite, and so it transcends the mind's capacities. Yet it 'abides in silence within our mind' because it comprehends all things within itself and is immanent in all things, and all things exist within it'" (81).

The Mystic Heart brought me to Interspirituality and subliminally paved the way for the time when abiding in silence would awaken me to my own mystic heart—to the lived experience of being a mystic.

The confluence of my Hindu teacher's grace, Fr. Bede's dream initiation, and a sincere and dedicated commitment to the practice of silence—fed especially by my many solo retreats at Sky Farm Hermitage in Northern California and the writings of my Naqshbandi Sufi teacher—deepened my recognition and acceptance of being an Interspiritual mystic.

The way of the mystic is the way of silence. As Sw. Shraddhananda implores the Beloved in the close of her poem:

> *speak me*
> *into silence*
> *silence me*
> *into love.*

The internationally beloved Benedictine monk, Br. David Steindl-Rast has written, "the heart of all ritual is stillness; the heart of all teaching is silence." My Hindu, Christian and Sufi teachers inspired me by their lives, their writings and their single-pointed devotion to the Sacred, but it was through their devotion to Silence that I learned the most. When one is silenced into love, what more can one say? One is no longer the subject of a Rumi poem; one is the poem itself, standing still and quiet as "the heart of all ritual…"

IV. Practical Implications Beyond the Nine Elements Retreat

Interspirituality and the SBNRSI

The Practical Mysticism of Reiki

Seva Arises from the Heart

Our Prayer for Planetary Transformation

Interspirituality and the SBNRSI

T. S. Pennington

I often label myself as Spiritual, But Not Religion Self-Identified. I do not have an external entity that I call "God." I generally do not participate in rituals or such practices as praying, chanting and reading scriptures. I am not a scientist, but I have an evolutionary mindset; therefore, I see the world through this framework. Despite my differences from Wayne Teasdale, who was Roman Catholic, the Nine Elements of Interspirituality outlined in his book *The Mystic Heart* are the guidelines on how I live my life. Here follows my interpretation of the Nine Elements.

1. Actualize and live my full moral and ethical capacity.

There is essentially agreement across all religious traditions about what is moral and ethical. A very similar understanding can be deduced using reason and logic. There are prohibitions against lying, stealing, killing and other harmful actions, but mostly in terms of dealing with other people.

Most religious traditions also include regulations about proper clothing, what should and should not be included in one's diet, and performing certain activities at various times of the year (i.e., observing religious holidays) which are unique to the faith tradition. They are moral and ethical for people in the faith tradition, but they are not universally appropriate. And they are important because a sense of ethics helps to give a tradition its unique identity.

2. Live in solidarity with the cosmos and all living things.

This element is core for me. My greatest heartbreak is the fact that the Earth is dying, and it is because of us, *Homo sapiens*. I have given myself the title of *Earth Witness*, a person who advocates the preservation of this planet. I believe that all of humanity needs to create and live into a new story of our interconnection with all that surrounds us. Personally, I believe anyone who attempts to live out of this element must have a fundamental understanding of cosmology and evolution. Chapters in the book *The Coming Interspiritual Age* by Dr. Kurt Johnson are devoted to these topics, and I have found them to be helpful.

Pierre Teilhard de Chardin, the French theologian, believed that evolution was God's method of creation. I wish people of all faith traditions could accept a similar understanding. If we shared some commonality in our creation stories, then it might be easier for us to live in solidarity with the Earth and each other.

3. Live in nonviolence.

Br. Teasdale used the word "deep" in front of nonviolence. My interpretation of "deep nonviolence" goes beyond physical (injuring or killing) to verbal and even to entertaining violent thoughts. Another aspect to this depth is in terms of the intended direction of possible violence. Besides nonviolence to other people, I would include nonviolence to oneself, to all living things, and even to non-living things. I see what humanity is doing to this planet as an act of violence. We must consume other life forms as well as the Earth's resources to live, but we must bring greater awareness to this consumption so that we live in a sustainable manner. We must accept that our survival is interconnected and interdependent on all that surrounds us.

4. Live in humility.

Although I have gained some wisdom over my lifetime, I realize that I do not have all the answers. What understandings I have gained are because of those who have gone before me; they have become my teachers and guides. I must speak my truth to the best of my ability, but I must also listen with an open mind and a loving heart to others. I believe that dialogue was so important to Br. Wayne, because it is an act of humility. If someone compliments me on what I say or do, then I need to remember that I have become who I am because of others. Often, what I say or write does not seem to come from my sense of ego/self, but an inner source that is beyond me. Humility also means that I should seek neither power nor praise for my accomplishments.

5. Embrace a daily spiritual practice.

There are a multitude of spiritual practices. Spiritual practices will vary from one individual to another. My practices include meditation, journaling, relating to the natural world and being in dialogue. I find being in an unguided, group meditation deeply satisfying.

I label myself as a contemplative. I feel that unless a person is extremely fortunate to have a spontaneous awakening, it is necessary to have daily contemplative practices to obtain and maintain the higher levels of spiritual development.

6. Cultivate mature self-knowledge.

Personally, this starts with being aware of my likes and dislikes, my skills and shortcomings, my strengths and weaknesses. But I am not isolated from my surroundings and from human biology and history. Cosmology and evolution are essential to my understanding of who I am. But fundamental knowledge of other sciences such as neurobiology, sociology, and transpersonal psychology need to be added for me to have adequate self-knowledge. These sciences show how human brain biology affects my behavior, how social interactions influence me in my actions and reactions, and how I conceive of myself and the world around me

I also need a model for developing spiritual maturity. I have studied various models such as James W. Fowler's Stages of Faith, Susan Cooke-Grueter's Nine Levels of Increasing Embrace, and Ken Wilber's Integral Theory and Integral Spirituality. As I reflect on my life, I see that I have gone through each of the stages, and they give me guidance about my future areas of growth as well as my challenges.

7. *Live a life of simplicity.*

To live a life of simplicity means that I do not let my lifestyle interfere with my spiritual development. Examples are the following: I don't schedule myself with so many activities that I do not find the time for daily spiritual practice; I don't have so many possessions that I spend lots of time and money accumulating and keeping care of them; I eat sustainably, lower on the food chain. For me, simplicity is closely linked to humility.

8. *Live a life of selfless service and compassionate action.*

This vow is the most difficult for me. I live almost as a hermit. It is difficult to be of service when one spends so much time in solitude. I will most often help when asked, but I do not go looking for opportunities to volunteer. I strive to be kind to other people and to the Earth. I am involved with ecological groups on the local and national level. Perhaps the best thing I can do living in solitude is to reflect on the human condition in the twenty-first century and to write and share my reflections with anyone who is interested.

9. Express the deepest realization of my inner practice through the prophetic call to work for justice, compassion and world transformation.

When I read *The Mystic Heart* back in the summer of 2007, my greatest heartbreak was that people of various religious traditions would use their differences as a valid reason to disdain, persecute, and kill those who were not of their tradition. This still deeply saddens me. I continue to believe in Br. Teasdale's idea that Interspirituality could bring peace between the various faiths by exploring the universal spirituality that makes up the core of all of them.

I am a strong advocate for many different social justice issues. But my greatest concern is with environmental justice. Unless humanity faces the global problems of climate change, overpopulation, sustainability, renewable energy, disposal of waste, etc., then the issues of social justice are moot points on a dead planet.

I am just beginning to explore and live into how to advocate, be a witness, and even a prophet for ecological justice. I am seeking guidance, teachers, colleagues and friends, because this great work cannot be done in isolation.

The Practical Mysticism of Reiki Healing

Dr. Joan "Kalisara" Dittrich

According to Br. Wayne Teasdale, "mystical spirituality is always *practical*: its experience is eminently beneficial to a person's life and well-being" (MH, 220). Mystical experience, whether it comes in the form of expanding consciousness, visionary messages, or spontaneous awakenings and healings, always benefits the one who has the experience. And in most cases, the benefits received by one ripple out in good works to others.

Teasdale explains that not only does mystical experience enlighten and elevate us to the transcendent, but it also is psychologically integrative and promotes what he refers to as "spiritual maturity." The mystic who sees the unity behind the patchwork quilt of life sees others compassionately and yearns for all beings to be well. Teasdale gives the example of Mother Teresa who had the ability to perceive the divine in everyone and was therefore compelled to work tirelessly for the unloved, the unwanted, the homeless and the dying. Mother Teresa exemplified the practical mystic.

Reiki as Practical Mysticism

Reiki is an ancient art of hands-on healing. Reiki, which means "universal life force energy," is spiritual energy mystically activated and perceived. And yet, Reiki is eminently practical. Its primary purpose is to heal or make whole that which is out of alignment with itself. What could be more practical than placing hands on yourself or another person to produce deep relaxation, physical and emotional healing, spiritual upliftment and balance? Who can deny the soothing effects of human touch? When that touch is infused with spiritual love through healing hands, it has been shown over and over again that people respond positively and that whatever hurts is eased or healed.

Even though Reiki energy itself cannot yet be directly observed or quantified, science has been able to measure its beneficial effects. This is why hospitals around the world are now inviting Reiki practitioners to offer hands-on healing for patients undergoing chemotherapy, wound and burn recovery, women's health issues, childbirth and various psychological disorders, including anxiety, depression, substance abuse and PTSD.

Reiki is an Interspiritual practice that in and of itself leads to mystical awakenings and inner transformation.

The Gift of Healing

Throughout history there have been reports of mysterious and spontaneous healings. Such healings have been attributed to forces of nature, gods, goddesses, saints, avatars, and "gifted" individuals. People pilgrimage in throngs to sacred healing sites such as Lourdes, Medjugorje, and Fatima. They travel the globe to receive the blessings and prayers of well known healers such as John of God in Brazil.

Jesus is probably the world's most well known healer. The word "savior" as ascribed to Jesus has as its Greek root, "soter," which can also be translated as "healer." Jesus healed the sick, restored vision to the blind, and life to those known to be dead. One merely had to be in his presence to receive healing. According to Sw. Shraddhananda, this healing energy that Jesus and other enlightened beings could bestow is called "Shaktipat," or the descent of divine energy through the grace of the guru (JWSG, 2).

Mikao Usui, a Pure Land Buddhist monk and the founder of traditional Usui Reiki, was likely one such "Shaktipat Guru." After a devastating earthquake in Japan in 1923, Usui and his students legendarily healed thousands simply by walking through the streets and offering Reiki healing to the injured and traumatized. The story of Usui's awakening is classic. After a 40 day fast and retreat on Mount Kurama near Kyoto, Usui had a profound mystical Kundalini experience in which Reiki life force energy poured into his crown chakra. As he walked down the mountain in this sublime state, a series of symbols were infused into his consciousness.

These symbols were understood by Usui to be divinely given tools he could use to teach others how to activate healing life force energy. Usui's school, Usui Shiki Ryoho, developed in 1922, as systematized hands-on healing methods for various disorders of body and mind. Thus, with the proper initiations and training in harnessing life force energy and hand placement protocols, anyone could become an effective healer of all variety of ailments.

Reiki, therefore, is a practical method based upon mystical revelation. Indeed, Usui himself was a practical mystic.

Universal Life Force

Usui taught that Reiki is the universal energy of the life force. "Rei" in Japanese means emperor or supreme, whereas "ki" is the life force. "Ki" is the same as the perhaps more familiar Chinese word for life force energy, "chi." Thus, Reiki is the supreme or divine energy of the life force. Life force energy is given many names in many traditions. In Yoga and Hinduism, it is "prana," "shakti," or "Kundalini." In the Judeo-Christian tradition it can be understood as "Shekinah," "Ruach," "Holy Spirit," or "Christ Consciousness." In African, Native American and shamanic cultures, there are many names for embodiment of the Great Spirit. In Muslim culture, it is the sublime consciousness, "baqa," or the remembrance of God, through the "ruqhyah" or healing words of the *Quran.*

To the modern scientist, life force is the hypothesized unified field. According to Teasdale, the unified field that has eluded physics is consciousness itself: "Consciousness is the unified field that brings everything together in itself, in the cosmic totality that grounds all creation" (3). Teasdale later declared that consciousness is nothing but love itself.

This is also the definition of Reiki energy, that Reiki life force is the substratum of all life and creation. Reiki healing is the intentional application of the life force to bring balance, wholeness, and healing to individuals and all the interacting systems that support life. This life force is mystically perceived by the Reiki practitioner as the pure light of consciousness, which is further perceived as divine love.

Because the energy of Reiki is universal, it is necessarily a practice that is Interspiritual in nature. The energy of Christian laying on of hands, for instance, is considered no different than the energy channeled by Buddhist monks or shamanic healers. Methods may vary from tradition to tradition, and varying methods may produce varying results, but the energy of healing is the source energy of that which gives us life and can renew and make us whole.

From Universal to Personal

One of the things I love about Reiki healing is its eminent simplicity. We simply tap into the energy of what we actually are in order to bring ourselves back into balance or alignment. In bringing our systems into attunement within ourselves and our environment, the body-mind relaxes, and the natural healing processes of the body are allowed to do their work. For example, studies show that Reiki helps to activate a suppressed immune system. How does this happen?

I like to understand it this way: by applying pure healing life force energy to energy that is clogged, congested or constricted, the stuck energy is freed up to flow naturally. It is like removing old tires dumped into a stream that obstruct the flow and pollute the water. When clogged energy corresponds to organs or tissues in the body, the freeing up of that energy allows the natural flow to resume. In the case of the immune system, glands and hormones may be purified and regulated so that the body can again ward off potential toxins. This process is simple and practical but ultimately mystical.

Any Reiki practitioner can give you anecdotal stories of dramatic healings with Reiki: an autistic child uttering his first words while receiving Reiki, tumors mysteriously disappearing after months of unsuccessful radiation and chemotherapies, suicidal depression giving way to states of radiant joy, a healthy child conceived and born to an anxious mother after multiple miscarriages and a stillbirth. One woman I worked with 20 years ago, when she was first diagnosed with non-Hodgkin's lymphoma and given less than five years to live, believes that her long remission is a result of the Reiki given so many years ago. Also, there have been many instances of tumors found on scans that disappear or shrink significantly after Reiki treatments.

It is not uncommon for clients on my table to have mystical experiences themselves. While receiving Reiki, they may sense the presence of angelic beings or deceased loved ones. Clients report that they have seen the eye of God and been visited by Christ or Buddha or Kali or Kwan Yin. They are often given messages and "travel" to fantastic mystical realms.

These seemingly extraordinary experiences happen frequently and consistently with Reiki healing. Because so many Reiki practitioners are mystics and not scientists, many of these miraculous events are not quantified or documented in any systematic way. Although there have been efforts in the last 20 years to research Reiki, these studies are typically not well funded and often do not hold up to the rigorous standards of scientific method, so remain primarily anecdotal.

I want to share with you here one very down to earth story of a very practical Reiki healing.

Bob is a giant of a man, a tradesman and mechanic who has done various jobs around my house, such as replacing appliances and fixing a broken pump. There doesn't seem to be anything that Bob cannot fix or make. Recently, after he moved some very heavy items, I saw the big guy wincing in pain. A little shy at first to offer my "woo-woo" services, I remembered my own observation that when people are in real pain, they will accept almost any form of help, regardless of whether it fits with their worldview.

So, I asked Bob if it would be okay for me to put

my hands on his shoulder. He nodded in ascent. Standing on my tiptoes, I reached up and held his shoulder between my Reiki-activated hands. Immediately, his expression softened, and his breathing got quieter. I doubt that he had ever meditated before, but he clearly was in the zone. After several quiet minutes, I sensed that the healing was complete and asked him how he was feeling. As if waking up from a deep sleep, he smiled beatifically and said the pain was gone completely.

A few weeks later he was back at the house, this time fixing my broken air conditioner. I asked him about his shoulder. He looked at me with amazement and said, "You know, I was completely pain free for three days, and the pain is still less than it has been for years. Nothing else, not medication or physical therapy, has ever done that. I want to know, what is it that you do?"

How do you explain the mysterious process of Reiki energy healing to someone who understands the world in mechanical terms? I simply said, "Well, Reiki is the energy of life. It is the energy we are all made of. When I place my hands on you and activate that energy, I am not giving you my energy. The energy that is activated in my hands simply activates the life force energy that is in you. And that allows your energy to re-boot itself and come into what is the healthiest alignment for you. In this case, it relieved your pain."

Bob was completely satisfied with my explanation. From now on, we are going to trade services when one of us needs something "fixed."

Mystical Origins, Practical Applications

When Reiki was introduced into the United States

after World War II, its Japanese Buddhist origins were often underplayed, as were its mystical elements. In an effort to westernize Reiki, false legends about Mikao Usui were promulgated, including that he went to divinity school in Chicago and that he developed Reiki in order to imitate the healing methods of Jesus. Research has found that Usui never visited the United States, and although he may have had respect for Jesus, he was simply a monk with a gift for healing who was mystically given a method that could teach others to become healers. Reiki's Buddhist origins made his practice suspect to various Christian organizations, including the Catholic Church whose Council of Bishops still officially condemns the practice of Reiki by its members. (This in spite of the fact that numerous Catholic priests and monastics, some of whom I am acquainted with, are long term Reiki practitioners who use Reiki when visiting the sick and in easing the death transition.)

In an effort to mainstream Reiki and render it accessible to the general public, it is often taught as a "non-religious" practice. The secularization of Reiki has, perhaps, made it more palatable to the medical community and facilitated its introduction into Western hospitals and other institutions. Indeed, Reiki can be practiced without referring to it in spiritual terms at all. This can make Reiki healing more acceptable to patients who would dismiss energy healing as either non-scientific or antithetical to various church doctrines.

While some Reiki practitioners prefer to think of it in completely pragmatic and non-spiritual terms, others like myself consider it a highly spiritual practice that belongs to no particular religious tradition. It is a truly Interspiritual practice that is available to anyone who is willing to learn. Reiki healing is complementary with all other genuine spiritual practice such as prayer, contemplation, and study of sacred texts.

Whereas Reiki can be taught without spiritual language, the ability to activate Reiki energy in one's hands, heart and mind involves a highly mystical initiatory process called an "attunement." Reiki attunements are initiations given only by Reiki master teachers, who were attuned by another master teacher, and so forth through the lineages.

What happens in an attunement is not shared with the general public, and the ritual process is not taught to the practitioner until she reaches a certain level of Reiki training, often considered Master Level. The process is reminiscent of ancient Mystery School rites and so is characterized by a very mystical passage. Students receiving an attunement often have visions of deities, angels, spirit guides, and may experience unitive consciousness. They often report a sense of coming "home" or knowing themselves as they truly are.

The attunement is a sort of *Shaktipat* initiation, or descent of grace that activates and empowers the student's natural healing abilities. The attunement process is what sets Reiki apart from other forms of energy healing. It is understood that the attunement process ensures that the practitioner will not re-absorb negative energies and that Reiki can only be applied for positive purposes, thus doing no harm. It also gives the student direct access to universal life force energy or what some call the Divine. As one practices Reiki more and more, one's understanding of the underlying wholeness of all being naturally expands.

Thus, although Reiki hands-on healing is assuredly practical, when its mystical origins are disregarded, one of its greatest boons, being a mystical path in and of itself, is at risk of being overlooked.

Reiki and Unitive Consciousness

Kurt Johnson and David Robert Ord (TCIA, 4) emphasize that all Interspiritual practices embrace unitive consciousness. Unitive consciousness is not merely an intellectual or poetic concept, but is the actual experience of oneness with all beings and indeed with all that is. It is the experience of being one with and not other than the source of everything.

The fully awakened human is one who in every moment can access this experience of the oneness of all beings and yet still function as a discrete being. Most of us do not live at this high level of consciousness most of the time, nor do we have easy access to it. We get lost in our activities, and in the contents of our minds, and we experience ourselves as separate and apart from others. For most humans, there are only occasional and brief glimpses into unitive consciousness. Precious moments at the birth of a child, gazing into the vastness of an ocean or night sky, the homecoming of a beloved, or the orgasmic gasp of union in lovemaking may provide these glimpses.

Reiki provides glimpses into unitive consciousness on a consistent and reliable basis for many of its practitioners. To feel energy emanating from myself that is not *my* individual energy but is the energy of the universal life force of which I am also made *and* to feel that energy connecting with the life force that flows through, within and as you, is a truly cosmic, unitive experience. This is mystical consciousness, and there is the possibility of experiencing it each time the practitioner places healing hands on someone in need. Indeed, the practitioner can experience this oneness even when sending Reiki to someone far away.

Reiki healing works across time and space. This

means that healing sent to someone across the globe can be just as effective as hands-on healing in the here and now. Clients I work with over the phone often report profound pain relief, deep relaxation, and release from emotional trauma. Sometimes they experience healing at the exact moment that I am sending life force energy, and sometimes they experience it either before or slightly after I have sent it. One time traveling in the Yucatan, a woman on my tour bus got extremely carsick. She disembarked from the bus and wandered off a little into the jungle. I, too, got off the bus and began walking toward her. When I got close to her, I offered her some hands-on Reiki, which she accepted. After a long time of having my hands on her, I asked if she was feeling any better. "Oh yes," she said, "the sickness went away as soon as you started walking toward me." I think that once her energy body sensed my intention to give her Reiki, she was healed. She hadn't really needed the hands-on treatment at all!

Both the Reiki healer and the receiver often experience a sense of timelessness and bodilessness during Reiki sessions. This sense of being completely aware without experiencing the anchors of time, space and egoic identity is characteristic of unitive consciousness. It is the great "*aham*" of the Yogic traditions, and the "I am that I am" of the Abrahamic traditions.

Chances are, most Reiki practitioners and their clients do not initiate their energetic healing work from a state of full enlightenment. Most people start receiving or practicing Reiki, because they are in some sort of discomfort. They are seeking relief from suffering. For the practitioner, Reiki is a technology that, glimpse by glimpse, allows entrance into the experience of universal life force energy and spiritual awakening. As for the Reiki recipient who finds relief from pain and suffering in a method that does not require physical or mechanical intervention, an entire new world view may begin to unfold.

Reiki as Spiritual Technology

In *The Mystic Heart*, Br. Teasdale says, "Daily spiritual practice is the 'technology' of inner change" (5). He goes on to enumerate transformative spiritual practices such as contemplative prayer, meditation, and sacred reading. He includes chanting, hatha yoga, certain martial arts, hiking and walking. I would include Reiki among those transformative practices.

As a daily practice, the Reiki practitioner spends quiet time in meditation and also in "self-healing," which entails activating Reiki healing energy and placing hands on oneself. This self-healing practice is considered essential to becoming a proficient Reiki healer. Reiki self-practice is a technology of individual evolution. It is a practice in self-compassion, and understanding that in order to serve others, we must care for our own body and spirit. Also, it is a purifying practice that readies the person to be a vessel of healing for others. Reiki self-practice assists the healer in being a pure channel of Reiki energy and averts the possibility of projecting one's own negativity onto another as well as preventing the healer from absorbing negative energy from the other.

As Mirabai Starr said during a conversation with Miranda McPherson on The Shift Network (2015), "Spiritual Practice is a means to prepare us for whatever may lie ahead." Reiki self-practice prepares the practitioner to move forward in the face of her own and others' unavoidable suffering, and to be an instrument of comfort and ease for those traveling dark roads.

In practicing Reiki on oneself and others, the Reiki healer gradually develops a fine-tuned intuition, and her healings grow in their effectiveness and potency, as confirmed by healing recipients. For some this developing intuition may mean increasing psychic abilities, including the ability to "see" a tumor or growth before it is confirmed through x-ray, or "reading" how old held traumas are contracting into physical or emotional pain. These abilities instruct the healer in how to work with a client and direct healing energy where it is needed.

Whereas these abilities are natural outgrowths of disciplined Reiki practice, they are also reminiscent of various Yogic "powers" or "siddhis" which are achieved through deep meditative practice, according to Book 3 of *The Yoga Sutras.* Healing itself is one of the siddhis attributed to deep practice, and great masters across all spiritual traditions have been natural healers. Reiki just happens to be a technology for developing the siddhi of healing. It is a technology that is available to everyone and is not limited to fully enlightened beings. This would seem to make it an ideal practice for the Interspiritual Age.

Reiki and Mature Interspirituality

As one grows in Reiki mastery, one naturally becomes attuned to the vows of mature Interspirituality as laid out by Teasdale in *The Mystic Heart.* I believe that most Reiki masters, whether or not they have made an overt declaration, are Bodhisattvas: those who vow to steadfastly abide on this earth in order to provide service and healing to all beings and systems as well as the earth itself.

Reiki practitioners take seriously the powerful gift of

healing that has been bestowed upon us, and we agree not to send Reiki where it may not be welcomed. We do not set our own intentions for the healing of other beings, but rather respect their intentions for their own healing. We understand that we have an ethical obligation to respect the rights of our clients to privacy and safe touch.

We get excited when a client heals, but we do not take the credit. We are humbled and grateful for the healing energy that we are simply channeling with healing intention. Similarly, we do not ignore the benefits and gifts of Western medicine, and we encourage our clients to employ all healing modalities that they find to be helpful. Although I am delighted that the woman with non-Hodgkin's lymphoma I mentioned earlier attributes much of her longevity to Reiki, she and I both agree that the medical intervention she has received throughout the years has also been necessary.

Because Reiki is the universal life force which is the substratum of all existence, we honor all created things and live in deep nonviolence with all that is. We respect differences, because we know the underlying non-difference between us all. We look deeply into who we are and the impact that we have on others. We strive to heal ourselves of our own self-serving shortsightedness and our fears of weakness. We strive to speak the truth of who we are. We are instruments of compassionate service, and our souls wish for all beings to experience optimal harmonic balance and integration on all levels of body, mind, spirit and environment.

There is a humble wisdom that naturally develops as we are entrusted with divine Reiki energy to use for the well-being of those who seek healing and wholeness. We begin to see that everything is the energy of the divine, and we begin to live more and more in awe and gratitude for that life force and our ability to see it as that which gives light to all.

The Practicing Mystic

In time, the Reiki practitioner begins to perceive the world in a whole new light. She begins to embody that light. Her rational, materialistic paradigm of understanding the world shifts as she experiences everything as consciousness. She comes to understand that since everything is energy, transformation and even transmutation of form and matter can occur through the energy of intention, thought, and alignment with the divine. The Reiki practitioner sees the potential and the underlying intention for all livings things to harmonize and co-exist and feels the universal propulsion of consciousness to experience itself as the divine energy of which it is composed. The practitioner does not linger in a transcendent cloud of bliss. To the contrary, she has deep empathy for the suffering of humanity and the earth, and she is committed to healing at every possible juncture.

Like a Bodhisattva, the seasoned Reiki practitioner's vow is to restore wholeness wherever it is needed through activating Reiki healing energy. She also assists in the transformation of that which has been dissolved or shattered through ignorance, neglect, abuse, or the natural processes of life, death, and re-birth. A true Reiki master is one who embodies and radiates Reiki energy through the light of her clear thoughts and compassionate actions— indeed, by means of her whole being.

People without a spiritual path who come to Reiki for healing may find their path and begin to experience everything as sacred. People already on a path may experience Reiki healing and recognize its utility in clearing physical and emotional obstacles to further spiritual growth. People who learn how to practice Reiki may discover a path as well as a tool to help those who have not otherwise found relief from pain, addiction, and trauma. As both a path and a tool, Reiki is eminently mystical and completely practical.

Seva Arises from the Perspective of The Mystic Heart

Acharya Sw. Prakashananda
aka The Right Rev. Christine Deefholts

Some of us gathered here today may be called to selfless service (what is referred to in Yoga circles as seva) through the practical offering of running a center for the Community of The Mystic Heart, either now, or at some point in the future.

The offering of seva is very subtle and has many facets. Many fruits also arise for us (though we do not seek them) if we are open to receiving them! Above all, offering seva is a journey of self-discovery, and an opening into the heart of the Divine.

I'd like to share a little of my own initial experience of this wonderful practice which, when understood, becomes the very fabric of life.

During the time when my family was young, I ran a meditation center for several years. This is how it came about.

Having dropped my connection with childhood Catholicism, I shifted into a state of spiritual suspension and began walking a path into the wilderness of unknowing, absorbing myself in the mundane business of outer life with a bit of voluntary work thrown in when I was able to offer it. I offered my work dutifully, but it was not enough. I felt disconnected from joy, and at times, fell into a deep depression which I later understood as a repressed anger toward myself and life.

One day I saw an advertisement for a Yoga class and was drawn to joining, hoping to find a little peace of mind. After three or so classes, I received a dramatic wake-up call. Actually, it was an extraordinary spiritual awakening, the awakening of the Holy Spirit (or Maha Kundalini Shakti as the sacred energy is known in Yoga).

One night, after my baby had been fed and settled, I lay down to rest. As I began to drift into sleep, an audible cracking at the base of my spine threw me back into the waking state again as waves of bliss and brilliant light began to shoot up my spine, flooding my whole being and pouring out around me through my head and hands. I had never been so alert. In my mind's eye, two images emerged from the light, pulsing to the rhythm of the in and out breath—on the in-breath, the living face of Jesus, on the out-breath, the archetypal logos of the Cosmic Christ, standing within the wheel of life and light.

The consequence of this experience was a total reorientation of my understanding, a paradigm shift which opened up my spiritual life again. I now understood what it must have felt like to be a student learning at the feet of the Beloved. For a short while, I had stepped into the Mystic Heart.

Of course, after this amazing opening up of my being, I wanted to remain consciously connected all the time with that sweet awareness of Divine love, but all too soon, the veils of my everyday world closed over again. I wanted to be back in paradise again and knew that I needed to connect with a living Master from whom I could learn what was going on. Otherwise, it would be easy for me to switch off the Divine light and lapse back into everyday existence.

Within a matter of days, something happened. How true the old Indian maxim: when the student is ready, the Teacher appears. I was invited to attend a meditation center and instantly connected with the presiding Teacher there, a realised Master of Meditation. The sense of welcome and home-coming was palpable.

Over the next few years, alongside my meditation practice, I trained as a hatha yoga teacher and taught classes in my local community. The closing session of each class offered relaxation and meditation. For inspiration, I drew practices from many different traditions, and my students took their practice into their everyday lives. One enthusiastic group eventually approached me to ask for the whole class to be turned over to meditation—we all loved it! The plan for the whole term of lessons came together effortlessly.

And yet, I was concerned that such heady success might lead us to settle for second best. I loved the fact that the group was so interested in my personal practice, and yet I did not want to offer my students a hodgepodge of assorted practices. Being in a position of authority can corrupt an un-baked student's head if one proceeds too hastily. So I wrote to my own Teacher and asked her if I could open a meditation center under her wing of protection. With her sanction, the opening of a center in my own home was a truly transformative experience.

This period in my life stretched me in so many ways. I thought that I had been offering my classes in a spirit of seva, or selfless service, and conducting my family life in the same way. Yet now, somehow, a deeper relationship with my inner life and others began to unfold.

First, this period of time heightened my commitment to service in my community.

Second, it taught me to manage my time more effectively. Juggling family and work commitments is never easy, and of course, the keys are balance and moderation as well as holding a loving, unconditional awareness in our relationships.

It taught me to fall into a place of love and trust, no matter what appeared to be happening on the outside.

It taught me how to handle difficulties. For that, I had to re-educate my preconceived ideas and recognise "difficulties" as challenges to be met. I also had to step back from my ego, which always wants to assert itself and its "answers." Stepping back allowed for fresh and more creative solutions to arise.

Above all, this period of "stretching" taught me to welcome the underlying grace of each moment—this grace which underpins all that is.

After the initial influx of interest, the numbers of people attending our meditation group dropped back to two or three attendees per week. This drop in attendance was disheartening and disproportionate to all the perceived effort and hard work that was poured into every week to enable the center to function. The preparation involved cleaning the house thoroughly from top to bottom; baking items for light refreshment afterwards as some people would arrive hungry straight from work; writing and presenting the programme for each evening; practising and providing music for chanting; preparing a bookshop area; restoring everything back to a family home afterwards.

After a year, I was exhausted. Those who dropped in enjoyed the programmes, yet were not committed to offering any kind of practical support. Juggling family life, business activities, hatha classes and the center single-handedly, was proving too much for one person.

So, I held a community meeting to explore the theme of offering selfless service in the center, and we began by invoking grace. This was really helpful as it took the emphasis of inspiration away from our egoic input, and placed it in the hands of the Divine. I did not like what emerged, but I accepted it. The process clarified the situation for each of us. Finally, everyone understood that no one else had the time or energy to offer any help. I thanked them and wished them well.

There was nothing more to be done. I made a decision to close down the center and let everyone know, including my Teacher. A week or so later, I was flabbergasted to receive a call from overseas, thousands of miles away, letting me know that my Teacher wished me to keep the center open. This instruction ran counter to the evidence I could see for keeping the center open!

"Okay," I said, hugely surprised. I put the phone down and spent quite some time in deep contemplation of this whole situation. When the Holy Spirit is awake in a person, such incidents take on greater significance. The Holy Spirit is a great Teacher and shows us through such dramas how to let go of our distortions and misperceptions. What was I being shown? Perhaps I needed to delve deeper? Who exactly was running the center? Was it me? Why did I think it was my decision to make on my own? Suddenly, I was blessed with an insight. I saw that I had fallen into busy-ness—and into a sense of doer-ship. Instead of letting the Divine handle the meditation center, I had taken it all on my own shoulders, thinking that "I" was the one in control.

Once I realised that I did not need to be in controller mode, I relaxed and jumped right back into my joyful, spontaneous heart again. We still held our meetings every week. They had become the heart of our household routine, and we welcomed them. The children were sometimes the only attendees, and that was just fine. I would adapt the programme in the moment if need be, and we would fall into ecstatic chanting. How the children loved to be involved in helping! They were great at offering seva! Even today, thirty years later, they remember their participation and experiences and are, in turn, instilling the values and natural joy they experienced then in their children.

During this retreat, we have been talking about closing "the gap" that Sw. Shraddhananda mentioned in her presentation. In my meditation center drama, the grace of the Teacher and the student working together closed the gap! The challenge dissolved. In time, other dear souls came along who were able to offer a deeper commitment together with a strong sense of community.

Through the lesson of surrender, I learnt the value of running a center. I learnt the secret of offering true seva. I realised that it was not about outcomes, and certainly not about how many people were attending, or any of the other mundane details.

It was much more about the refining process of seva on the ego, and about enabling the freedom of joy which comes from a pure offering. The whole point of the effort expended, I saw, was to fall into my own center and, amid the busy-ness of life, hold a seat of silent joy in my heart.

My Teacher once offered a beautiful statement when speaking about seva. She instructed students to offer service with a pure heart. Selfless service produces a deep alchemy of transformation, she said.

So here we have it. When we offer whatever may come up in our lives from the perspective of the Mystic Heart, then all our goals, both mundane and spiritual, are beautifully fulfilled.

Our Prayer for Planetary Transformation

'Our prayer then becomes a belief in our ability to use prophetic voice for planetary transformation.'

Rev. JoAnn Barrett

In the midst of a brilliant and inspiring conference, I was surprised when I was asked to add my comments to a session serving as a kind of wrap-up during which Dr. Darrol Bryant and Yanni Maniates generously offered to share their presentation time with Patricia O'Connor and me. Patti and I were representing our community on Long Island in New York, Gathering of Light Interspiritual Fellowship. Although we have our own congregation on Long Island, we were inspired to be among those we believe to be true pioneers in the field of spiritual development, mainly under the heading of Interspiritual. Our purpose was to take back as much information as possible on Br. Wayne Teasdale's Nine Elements from our presenters and from retreat conversations.

In true Interspiritual style, I was asked to share my personal spiritual journey before offering feedback on the lead presentations. Being a heart centered spiritual path, Interspiritual discussions at this retreat focused on the innermost calling of the spiritual journeys for individuals who were present. There was sincere interest in my personal journey. The approach was holistic and supported the idea which contends that all parts are valuable to the whole. In line with a true evolutionary process in which each previous contribution is integral to the development of the current one, my story mattered. I was in attendance. I was respected. I have a unique voice to add to the ongoing process and development of Interspirituality. This generous spirit was offered to all participants although time did not allow for everyone to share in detail.

I reported that I was the daughter of immigrant Irish Catholic parents. I grew up in the Bronx, and the development of my spirituality was a journey into my heart rather than an expression of the religion of my birth. While I was schooled in Roman Catholic doctrine, my spirituality grew in the quiet moments I spent inside empty churches and in my communion with the solitary tree at the end of our city block.

The vibrant diversity which New York City afforded opened me to questioning. I frequently recall learning my colors for the first time. I understood that I was seeing blue, but my question was, "Is the blue that I am seeing the same as the blue that you are seeing? Can we all be saying the same thing but experiencing something different?" Interspirituality supposes that even in a Catholic mass, each individual can be having a uniquely personal relationship with the Divine. I always had a relationship with Jesus, but it was never the same Jesus that the church was teaching me about. The graphic crucifixion that dominated the center of church life depicted suffering and sacrifice. The Jesus I felt in my heart wanted only love for me and for me to be loving to others as well.

Interspirituality is a heart centered philosophy that integrates a sense of the sacred with the personal heart of each individual. The Nine Elements are guideposts to developing that which has already been bursting to come forth. My yearnings found beauty in practices from all over the neighborhood despite my upbringing which urged me to stay close to a constricted version of exclusivity. One would think that my resiliency was developed as a result of growing up in a rough neighborhood like the Bronx, but it was the pain in my heart that toughened me.

My family eventually moved out of the city to a town called Kings Park on Long Island, New York. Their goal was to provide a "safe" environment for our growth. While Long Island was certainly more homogenized than the Bronx, there were woods and lots more trees than the single one at the end of the block. A river also flowed through the area. My connection to nature flourished.

The move also opened up my perspectives as I now attended public school. But it wasn't until high school and my attendance in a class on World Religions that my heart was given a new course to traverse for blossoming. I learned about religious ideas that were different from the Roman Catholicism on which I was raised, and I was intrigued. But, the intellectual knowledge was just an appetizer. I wanted an experience of what I was learning. I signed up for Yoga classes, Zen meditation, and macrobiotic cooking classes. I explored temples and workshops. I spent nights in the woods absorbing the very ground of Mother Earth. My path was evolving, but somewhere deep in my heart, I was lonely.

I felt driven to pursue something, but I didn't know what I was searching for. I continued to explore all types of spirituality. I knew I was changing; I felt an unfolding but was uncertain as to how that would manifest. After privately studying *A Course in Miracles* workbook, I reached lesson 50, and my whole body began to shake. I knew deep down inside that if I continued to do these lessons, I would never be the same. Fear gripped me along with the haunting question, "what would I become?" My family was afraid that I would run off and join a cult. They told me I would turn out to be pathetic; I would wind up selling roses in airports. However, the intensity of the spiritual awakening I experienced while studying *A Course in Miracles* was so powerful that I knew I would be completely transformed— and I would be fine.

Later in my life, through a series of coincidences, I became an Interfaith minister and started Gathering of Light Multifaith Spiritual Fellowship. At Gathering of Light, we connect to the energy of the calendar of the World's Religions to choose weekly topics and "flavors" for our services. We learn new concepts from various spiritual systems. But mostly, we focus on spiritual principles associated with the holy days from different faiths.

Gathering of Light was never called an Interfaith fellowship despite my title as Interfaith Minister, because the energy of the spirit that was leading us was not exactly Interfaith. It was more than just different faiths or various theologies or collaborating on social causes. We were inspired by all the world's faith traditions to open our hearts and learn.

At Gathering of Light, we go beyond traditional faiths to spiritual philosophies like those in *A Course in Miracles* and the 12 Step programs. We feel called to gather positive, practical tools for purposes of continuing to grow spirituality. We are modern mystics, exploring and then challenging what evolves in our hearts as authentic spiritual expression. Each week at our services, we create universal experiences of spiritual connection through music, meditation and an inspirational message. The community has always been led by an energy that is expressed and confirmed by the participants who attend. In other words, it becomes more of what it is meant to be by the lights that gather and shine their lights within it. I began this community in 1996, three years before I encountered the word, *Interspirituality.* Today our community calls itself, Gathering of Light Interspiritual Fellowship.

This historic retreat on the Nine Elements of Interspirituality was of paramount importance to me as leader of a community that came into being three years before Br. Wayne Teasdale published *The Mystic Heart.* Since 2013 when Kurt Johnson and David Robert Ord's book entitled *The Coming Interspiritual Age* was published, we have drunk in every syllable of the title and the text. It was important for us to discover that we were not alone—and that we could see through the trees to what we would become by following this path. We hosted book club discussions on *The Mystic Heart.* We held workshops on *The Coming Interspiritual Age.* We even held three series on the Nine Elements in which we broke them up into nine different services for the summer months. This structure provided our community with an elementary introduction to the elements wrapped in songs and a meditation to accompany each one. We were bold and creative. We were part of a larger spirit that our input fed and helped to create.

All that being said, it was with great expectation that I listened to the presentations. Sw. Shraddhananda began with the first three elements. Her perspective came from a background that is different from mine, so I listened carefully. She began with the first two elements which primarily address ethics. It is important that we live as persons with an actualized moral capacity, Br. Teasdale wrote, and Sw. Shraddhananda talked about some of the problems facing a culture in which, according to Dr. Sigmund Freud, the "super ego," or psychic apparatus which distinguishes right from wrong, is diminished. Civilization, itself, is responsible for some of this "blurring" of ethics, Sw. Shraddhananda said, and especially in

Postmodern times beginning after World War II, it has become increasing difficult for each one of us to internalize an "infallible" sense of right and wrong.

Likewise, historically, having become fragmented as individuals and cultures, we have been faced with the ominous task of finding our way back to a sense of solidarity with other beings. Now, as we move toward greater awareness and understanding of spiritual truths, we gain a deeper awareness of our interdependence on each other.

Sw. Shraddhananda talked about the "gap" that sometimes exists between the values and the behavior of individuals. She cited Ernest Kurtz's book, *Not-God: A History of Alcoholics Anonymous*. Since Gathering of Light incorporates the 12 Step programs into our Interspiritual approach, here was a title and an idea I could take back to our group.

I was following along with the first two elements nicely, even though I had to "translate" Sw. Shraddhananda's frame of reference into my own. When we arrived at the third element, which is a commitment to deep nonviolence, a challenge began for me.

Sw. Shraddhananda had published a new book entitled *A Short Book about Killing*. This book pays tribute, she said, to the great Polish filmmaker Krzysztof Kieslowski whose 10-part *Decalogue* is based loosely on the 10 Commandments. Okay, I thought, that fits with Br. Teasdale's emphasis on the development of moral capacity.

Then, Sw. Shraddhananda read "Letter to a Jihadist from a Heathen," the last chapter in *A Short Book about Killing*. I had difficulty with the way she was using the term "jihadist." Through my encounters with Jain friends over the years at Gathering of Light, I learned that true nonviolence goes beyond restraint of outward obvious acts of violence. It includes inner ones as well.

I took Sw. Shraddhananda to task. Then, I realized that cutting someone off is itself an act of violence. An inner act of violence can be not listening in conversation to another's point of view. When we spend the whole time that someone is speaking to us deciding how we are going to respond, we may be setting ourselves up to commit a violent act. A heart centered spirituality cares for all and respects opinions different from our own. I was not opening my heart to Sw. Shraddhananda's perspective, and I had my own preconceived notions as to the usage of the word "jihadist." I had some work to do. After her presentation, we talked, and I was able to see her viewpoint.

Mirabai Starr's work has always intrigued me, so I was eager to hear her version of elements four, five, and six. My daily work taking care of the mechanics of our organization is very business-like, so Mirabai's poetic interpretation of the middle three elements was most welcomed.

Mirabai's presentation began with the importance of opening ourselves to humility. In our shadow and in our greatness, we are all still in this together. What a beautiful element for Mirabai to share. She read from her book *God of Love* which I decided immediately should be part of everyone's required Interspiritual reading list. I was humbled by the intensity of both her personal spiritual journey and her ability to express it. Her personal stories of the depth of her spiritual practices and the growth that ensued through them inspired a deeper commitment within me. Through her insight, I contemplated how to embrace an individual spiritual practice to which I could be vigilant. The spiritual journey necessitates the continued use of spiritual tools.

Mirabai's reflections on her journey through grief exacerbated by the death of her daughter took my breath away. Her latest book, *Caravan of No Despair*, illustrates beautifully her journey beyond despair to hope. Her ability to absorb healing from the sacred wherever she finds it is a testament to the Interspiritual spirit. Like Mirabai, I am a mother, the mother of six children, four by birth and two stepchildren. Every part of motherhood develops a keen sense of the importance of maturity. Despite my role as mother, my process of maturity requires me to, "let go and let God." It is amazing how the process of telling our stories in a raw and vulnerable way cultivates a mature self-knowledge and radical self-acceptance. The Interspiritual journey truly is a journey to "know thy Self."

Through all our individual processes, Interspiritual sojourners strive for lives of simplicity. We respect that the resources of the Earth are for all. At first, I could not see how Kurt Johnson embodies simplicity. He has a brilliant mind that not only comprehends complexities, but also has the capacity to articulate them. His sharing of the history of Interspirituality and the gatherings at Snowmass created a foundation for us to understand what has come to be called Interspirituality. Kurt's complex reports of conferences and gatherings, accomplishments and dialogues between Br. Teasdale and Fr. Bede Griffiths culminated for me in a single moment, when Kurt's eyes grew wide with wonder and awe at the sharing of personal items that belonged to Br. Teasdale. Kurt's admiration for Br. Teasdale and his contemporaries created a moment that was alive and present and very simple.

All the presenters at the Nine Elements retreat lead exemplary lives of inclusion and outreach. In our understanding and development, we work towards leading lives of selfless service and compassionate action. In our community, Gathering of Light, our motto is to "show up for each other," and it is important that we move beyond our own community to be of service to the greater community. Our Interspiritual fellowship collects soups to replenish food pantries during the Winter. In the Spring, we do recycling drives, and we grow a garden of fresh vegetables to share with those in need. Every year, we collect over 100 backpacks filled with school supplies for needy children in our area. We bake homemade pies for the homeless shelters. We adopt families in domestic violence centers. We annually collect Bedding for Babes. This program in the spirit of Toys for Tots is a collection of bed sets for children in homeless and DV shelters. They provide fun, comfort, and a sense of stability and safety in the facilities where children live. Our ongoing project is a Family Relocation essentials program. This unique program fills a gap in services in our area by providing families moving out of homeless shelters with basic household tools to promote independence in their new lives.

When Kurt described the work of others in the Interspiritual world, our projects immediately came to mind. As he shared the vision of the initial sojourners of Interspiritual ideals, I heard the last element come alive. As part of the evolutionary process of the globalization of our planet, speaking out with one's prophetic voice is necessary. The process of spiritual work transformed me. This transformation allowed me to build a spiritual community around me that attracts like-minded individuals who continue to grow spiritually. Together we expand our intuitive abilities and gather our lights together to support and encourage each other. *Our prayer then becomes a belief in our ability to use prophetic voice for planetary transformation.* Each of us has a unique gift to offer to the healing of the world.

Both Patti and I gathered much inspiration and knowledge from the presenters and through the exercises in which we participated during the retreat. I am happy to report, in summary, that the concept called Interspirituality exists in reality and that people need to hear more about it. Every avenue of exposure needs to be explored. This first residential retreat helped to establish a lineage of Interspirituality and in-depth inquiry into the Nine Elements, anchored for Gathering of Light Interspiritual Fellowship in a larger international community. Now, our laity can invite neighbors to participate in our group without feeling we are limiting them to our services alone. We can invite friends to explore a larger movement with its own texts and principles that live beyond our walls.

We conclude each service at Gathering of Light with the following benediction, so please allow me to offer it to help close our retreat: "We are grateful for the opportunity to witness the Divine in each other and trust that our showing up is another step towards peace on earth as we share peace words and words of religious greeting to all... *Om Shanti, Shalom, Salaam, Peace, Pax, Guru Rakha, Jai Jinendra, Blessed Be, He Ping, Amahoro, Aquene, Namaste, Pace, Aho!*"

V. Afterword

Looking for Interspirituality: An Afterword

Dr. M. Darrol Bryant

It was late April in 2016 when I set out from my home in southern Ontario for a retreat that was being held at the Boat Dock Road Retreat House in Somerset, Kentucky. It was a retreat of the Community of The Mystic Heart (CMH). I knew little or nothing about this group except that a couple of long-time friends, Kurt Johnson and Yanni Maniates, were involved and had invited me to join them. Kurt, an entomologist and social activist, had published *Nabokov's Blues*, on butterflies, and more recently, the widely acclaimed *The Coming Interspiritual Age*, together with David Robert Ord. It led us to get reacquainted. Yanni and I had worked together in the 1980s on some remarkable Interfaith conferences before he headed off into his own practice of spirituality. His *Magical Keys to Self-Mastery: Creating Miracles in Your Life* was the first of many contributions he has made to the practice of spirituality. They were friends. How could I say no to their invitation?

It took me a day and a half to make the drive. While traveling, I was seeing the world waking up to Spring. Leaves were not out in Elmira when I left home but as I drove into northwestern Pennsylvania, and then headed south, the promise of spring became increasingly visual…buds, then hints of leaves, and then as I entered West Virginia, there were young leaves. And when I arrived in the Cumberland Valley in Kentucky, it was spring time: flowers were out and the leaves were full.

But all during the drive I kept wondering what lay ahead? What did this Interspirituality look like? For decades, I had been engaged in Interreligious encounter and dialogue. I knew about Interfaith. Was this just a new name for the same old, for me, thing? It sounded to me like something beyond what I knew. And that was what I felt when I read Kurt's book. It was also something that came through in Wayne Teasdale's *The Mystic Heart: Discovering a Universal Spirituality in the World's Religions*. It had been part of my assigned reading for the forthcoming retreat. I had known of Wayne Teasdale ever since 1993 and the Parliament of the World Religions in Chicago. Like Teasdale I had been inspired by Abhishiktananda, the French Benedictine who had immersed himself in the Hindu Way and Bede Griffiths, who succeeded Abhishiktananda at Shantivanam in South India. Since the early 1980s, I had engaged the Hindu, Muslim, Sikh and Tibetan Buddhist communities in India, so I knew something of the transformative power of such meeting, and listening, and learning. But was this Interspirituality? I wondered.

In *The Mystic Heart*, Teasdale had called for a "Universal Order of Sannyasa"—"an Interspiritual order of monastics or contemplatives"—that would be open to all. But he was not able to realize his dream prior to his untimely death. Kurt picked up the mantle and was central to the founding of the Community of The Mystic Heart Order.

Teasdale recommended it be built around the following vows:

Marks/Vows of The Mystic Heart

I vow to actualize and live according to my full moral and ethical capacity.
I vow to live in solidarity with the cosmos and all living beings.
I vow to live in deep nonviolence.

I vow to live in humility and to remember the many teachers and guides
who assisted me on my spiritual path.
I vow to embrace a daily spiritual path.
I vow to cultivate mature self-knowledge.
I vow to live a life of simplicity.
I vow to live a life of selfless service and compassionate action.
I vow to be a prophetic voice as I work for justice, compassion, and
world transformation.

Was this the community I would be meeting? I
wondered.

The Boat Dock Road Retreat House was part of the
Slate Branch Ashram headed by Swami Shraddhananda.
Earlier known as the Rev. Dr. Sonya Jones, a Ph.D. from
Emory and a long-time Professor of World Religions in the
Honors Program at the University of Kentucky, she was our
gracious host. As I stepped out of my car into the warm and
sunny spring day, I was greeted and welcomed by the
Swamiji and most of the other 20 folks that would be part
of the retreats. It was a good beginning.

There were 15 women and 5 men. They came from
across the United States: California, New York, North
Carolina, New Mexico, Pennsylvania, etc. Three came from
Great Britain. They were yoga teachers, Interfaith ministers,
a doctor, seekers, and teachers. But no one introduced
himself or herself to me by mentioning a particular religious
tradition.

Over the three days, we talked, prayed, meditated,
engaged in some yogic stretches, listened to Kurt, Mirabai,
and Swamiji as they spoke about Teasdale's vision and their
spiritual journeys, shared meals, went for walks, engaged in
some spiritual practices and were together in silence. People
shared what they knew from their experience, no one

presented himself or herself as a spokesperson for a particular religious tradition. I realized that they had all been touched and influenced by a wide variety of practices and teachers coming from across the world's religious/spiritual traditions. And if they heard something or were taught a practice that enhanced their spirituality, they simply adopted it and integrated it into their life.

There was an utter absence of any sense of uneasiness arising from diversity or difference. And an openness towards one another that made the retreat so rich and enriching.

As I began the journey home, I found myself smiling to myself as I recalled moments from the days we had spent together. And I realized that I now had a living example of Interspirituality. It had been a gift, a Spring that brought something new into my life.

Bibliography

M. Darrol Bryant. *Assembly of the World Religions*. Paragon House. 1986.

_____, ed. *Huston Smith: Essays on World Religion*. Paragon House. 1995.

_____. *Religion in a New Key: Three Lectures*. Wiley Eastern. 1992.

_____. *Woven on the Loom of Time: Many Faiths and One Divine Purpose*. Decent Books. 1999.

Sigmund Freud. *Civilization and Its Discontents*. W.W. Norton & Company. 1989.

Kurt Johnson and Stephen H. Blackwell. *Fine Lines: Vladimir Nabokov's Scientific Art*. Yale University Press. 2016.

_____ and Steven L. Coates. *Nabakov's Blues: The Scientific Odyssey of a Literary Genius*. McGraw-Hill. 2001.

_____ and David Robert Ord. *The Coming Interspiritual Age*. Namaste Publishing. 2013. (TCIA).

Sonya Jones (now Sw. Shraddhananda). *Small Claims, Large Encounters*. Brito & Lair. 1995.

Ernest Kurtz. *Not-God: A History of Alcoholics Anonymous*. Hazelden Publishing. 1991.

Yanni Maniates. *Magical Keys to Self-Mastery: Creating Miracles in Your Life*. Masters Press. 2007.

Wendy Doniger O'Flaherty, tr. *The Laws of Manu*. Penguin Classics. 1992.

Jim Rosemergy. *The Third Coming*. Inner Journey. 2000.

Sw. Shraddhananda aka Rev. Dr. Sonya Jones. *Jesus Was a Shaktipat Guru*. The Sacred Feet Publishing Imprint. 2014. (JWSG)

_____. *A Short Book about Killing*. The Sacred Feet Publishing Imprint. 2016.

Mirabai Starr. *Caravan of No Despair: A Memoir of Loss and Transformation*. Sounds True. 2015.

_____. "Conversation with Miranda McPherson." The Shift Network. 2015.

_____. *God of Love: A Guide to the Heart of Judaism, Christianity and Islam*. Monkfish Book Publishing. 2012.

_____. *Saint Teresa of Avila: Passionate Mystic*. Sounds True. 2013.

Mukunda Stiles. *Yoga Sutras of Patanjali*. Wiser Books. 2001.

Wayne Teasdale. *A Monk in the World*. New World Library. 2003.

_____. *Bede Griffiths: An Introduction to His Interspiritual Thought*. SkyLight Paths. 2003.

_____. *The Mystic Heart: Discovering a Universal Spirituality in the World's Religions*. New World Library. 1999, 2001, 2010. (MH)

Ken Wilber. *Integral Spirituality: A Startling New Role for Religion in the Modern and Postmodern World*. Shambhala. 2007.

Biographies

Rev. JoAnn Barrett

Rev. JoAnn Barrett was ordained an Interfaith Minister in 1995. She has a master's degree in Social Policy, an undergrad degree in Human Services, and a credentialed degree in Substance Abuse Counseling. She is the founder of Gathering of Light Interspiritual Fellowship, CoChair of Interfaith Anti Bias Task Force of Suffolk County, a member of Suffolk County Hate Crimes Task Force, and a member of Peace Island Institutes Center of Interfaith Studies advisory board. A member of Religions for Peace Long Island (a local branch of a world-wide NGO at the United Nations), she is a member of the "Dignity for All Students Act" Committee which helped this bill pass in the NY State Senate. She is a member of the Huntington Clergy Association and a teacher of *A Course in Miracles* since 1980. She founded a community service project, "Lightworks," including Starter Packs for the homeless. She has been Pastoral Care Associate for North Shore, Syosset and Huntington Hospital and Clinical Director for a major LI substance abuse and addiction treatment center. She performs personalized wedding ceremonies for couples and has created rituals for all life events for hundreds of people. She has made public spiritual presentations at institutions including Stony Brook School of Social Welfare, and VA Medical Center. She is a published author and poet. She is married and has six grown children.

Dr. M. Darrol Bryant

Dr. M. Darrol Bryant received his B.A. in Philosophy and Political Science from Concordia College in Minnesota,

USA, his S.T.B. from Harvard Divinity School, Harvard University, USA, and his M.A. and Ph.D. from the Institute of Christian Thought at the University of St. Michael's College in the University of Toronto, Canada. Teaching since 1967, Dr. Bryant is Distinguished Professor Emeritus of Religious Studies and Founder/Director of the Centre for Dialogue & Spirituality in the World's Religions at Renison University College of University of Waterloo in Waterloo, Ontario, Canada. Deeply involved in and a notable contributor to Interfaith dialogue in the world's religions, he has authored *Huston Smith: Essays on World Religion*; *Woven on the Loom of Time: Many Faiths and One Divine Purpose*; and *Assembly of the World's Religions*, among other noteworthy texts. Ever since his childhood on the plains of North Dakota near a Native American reservation, Darrol has been keen to know more about his own Christian faith and the faiths of others. That passion has continued and deepened through his studies and through many opportunities to meet people of different faiths in their own settings—e.g., in ashrams, temples, masjids and gurdwaras in India, in Buddhist monasteries in Korea, Sri Lanka and Japan, and in masjids in Egypt and Turkey. He founded Spiritual Heritage Education Network Inc. (SHEN) in the hope that it becomes a resource and a place of dialogue about the wisdom essential to a life of spiritual depth.

Dr. Joni "Kalisara" Dittrich

Dr. Joni Dittrich aka "Kalisara" is a clinical psychologist, healer, and teacher of Reiki, yoga and meditation. She considers herself to be a "practical mystic" in that her work is based both in science and direct experience of the numinous. Joni has developed a psychotherapeutic technique, DROPPP (Deep Release of Persistent Pain

Patterns) which involves somatic and energetic release of trauma and long held negative thought and behavior patterns. A Reiki Master in four lineages, Joni is a powerful healer and the founder of Kali-Ki Reiki and Wisdom School®, dedicated to the direct exploration of consciousness. Kali-Ki Reiki® is an energetic and shamanic method for healing the self and others and a path to spiritual awakening. This new lineage emerged from Joni's deep immersion in the divine feminine within world mystical traditions and her own experience. Joni studied Theology at Vanderbilt Divinity School and earned her doctorate in Psychology from the University of Memphis. She has studied Reiki with her Master Teacher Connee Pike, William Rand, and Anne Uemura, Ph.D. She has studied meditation with Paul Muller-Ortega for 10 years and is grateful to all teachers along the way. She was ordained as an Exorcist in the Liberal Catholic Movement in April 2017 by Bishop Christine Deefholts aka Sw. Prakashananda.

Dr. Kurt Johnson

Dr. Kurt Johnson has worked in professional science and comparative religion and culture for over 40 years. He serves on many international committees, particularly at the United Nations. A leader in the Interspiritual Movement, he heads the Community of The Mystic Heart and has worked tirelessly on behalf of Bro. Wayne Teasdale's legacy. Author of the acclaimed *The Coming Interspiritual Age* (Namaste, 2013), Dr. Johnson is recognized internationally for his work in science and spirituality. He has published over 200 scientific articles, is a regular presenter at The Science and Nonduality Conference, and his text entitled *Fine Lines* (Yale, 2016) was named a Top 20 book in the sciences for 2016. For 25 years, Dr. Johnson served on staff at the

American Museum of Natural History, and for over a dozen years, he has taught classes at One Spirit Learning Alliance in New York City. He directed sessions featuring Deepak Chopra and other luminaries for the Convergence series of VoiceAmerica online talk radio; he works with 1God Academy and is scheduled to teach Interspiritual Studies for The Anugraha Institute. He holds a Ph.D. in Evolution, Ecology, and Comparative Biology from the Graduate Center at City University. See David Sloan Wilson's Evolution of the Coming Interspiritual Age: A Conversation with Kurt Johnson.

T. S. Pennington

T. S. Pennington is a retired college instructor of computer science. He graduated from One Spirit Interfaith Seminary in 2008. He was inducted into the Community of The Mystic Heart at the first ceremony in Washington D.C. in January 2010. He served as a member of CMH leadership circle for three years. He now lives just outside of Asheville, North Carolina.

Acharya Sw. Prakashananda
aka The Right Rev. Christine Deefholts

Acharya Sw. Prakashananda Saraswati aka Rev. Chris Deefholts is a disciple of the Siddha lineage and a member of the Saraswati Order of Monastics as well as the Community of The Mystic Heart Sannyasa. She has been appointed Presiding Bishop of the Mission Episcopate of the Holy Spirit based in the United Kingdom. Sw. Prakashananda studied Vedanta with Sw. Anubhavananda for fifteen years. She also studied Tibetan Buddhism with Lama Gangchen for several years. She received Sannyas and was ordained as a Sacred Feet Yoga Acharya by Sw.

Shraddhananda. Sw. Prakashananda plans to incorporate The Five Teachings of Sacred Feet Yoga into her work to enhance understanding of the Holy Spirit or Maha Kundalini Shakti, particularly among Christians, in England. She lives in the United Kingdom where she has worked as a healer, a Hatha Yoga teacher, and a bookseller in Oxford. A graduate of the University College London, she was certified in Hatha Yoga with distinction by the Friends of Yoga—All India Board, and is a Doctoral Fellow at the Anugraha Institute. She has three grown children, five granddaughters and a grandson.

Rev. Dr. Sw. Shraddhananda

Rev. Dr. Sw. Shraddhananda Saraswati, as its founder, serves as Provost and CEO of The Anugraga Institute for Yoga and Interspiritual Studies. She has published numerous articles and books, most recently *Jesus Was a Shaktipat Guru* (Sacred Feet, 2014) and *A Short Book about Killing* (Sacred Feet, 2016). Sw. Shraddhananda has a long history in academic teaching dating back to Allegheny College, a select plus liberal arts institution where she was tenured and promoted to full professor, followed by the Honors Program at the University of Kentucky and service as the first Dean of Graduate Studies at The New Seminary. She has studied Yoga since 1988 as a disciple of the Siddha lineage as it manifests in Bhagawan Nityananda of Kanhangad and Ganeshpuri. In 2010, she received transmissions for the founding of Sacred Feet Yoga, an Interspiritual path which she heads as disseminator of Shaktipat, the sacred energy known as the Holy Spirit in Christianity. She is also a lifelong Christian, and for eleven years, she meditated and studied with the Shambhala Buddhists. She attended Warrior Assembly and is a

Registered Shambhala Buddhist Guide. Sw. Shraddhananda currently serves as Preceptor and Lineage Holder of the Sannyasa prong of the Community of The Mystic Heart, an Interspiritual community anchored in the teachings of Br. Wayne Teasdale. With the approval of the Mahamandaleshwar, she also offers Sannyas in the Saraswati Order of Monastics dating back to Shri Shankaracharya in 8th century India. She is an ordained Exorcist in the Liberal Catholic Movement. She holds a Ph.D. from Emory University. She has lectured on six continents.

Acharya Sandra "Chamatkara" Simon

Acharya Sandra Chamatkara Simon was the first Acharya ordained in the Sacred Feet Yoga tradition as well as the first certified teacher of Sacred Feet Hatha Yoga. She has attended every Sacred Feet Yoga retreat since the initial one held at Slate Branch Ashram in 2011. She opened the first Sacred Feet Yoga Meditation Center in Pittsburgh, Pennsylvania in 2014, and she has taught with Sw. Shraddhananda in several retreats. Acharya Chamatkara currently serves as Managing Editor of The Sacred Feet Publishing Imprint. She taught herself how to make a book for purposes of publishing Sw. Shraddhananda's *Jesus Was a Shaktipat Guru*. After being named the first Chaitanya Fellow in Doctoral Studies at The New Seminary, Acharya Chamatkara elected to continue doctoral studies as a Fellow at The Anugraha Institute. Acharya Chamatkara lives in Pittsburgh where she works as office manager for a company that matches attorneys with employers. She graduated from Allegheny College in 2000.

Mirabai Starr

Mirabai Starr writes creative non-fiction and contemporary

translations of sacred literature, especially the Spanish mystics, John of the Cross (*Dark Night of the Soul*) and Teresa of Avila (the *Interior Castle* and the *Life*). She taught Philosophy and World Religions at the University of New Mexico-Taos for 20 years and now teaches and speaks internationally on contemplative practice and Interspiritual dialog. Mirabai met Ram Dass in 1975 at the Lama Foundation when she was fourteen, and has been a devotee of Neem Karoli Baba ever since. Her newest book, *CARAVAN OF NO DESPAIR: A Memoir of Loss and Transformation,* dedicated to Ram Dass, received the Spirituality & Practice "Best Books of 2015" award. *GOD OF LOVE: A Guide to the Heart of Judaism, Christianity & Islam,* was also the winner of numerous awards. She lives with her extended family in Taos, New Mexico, home to the Hanuman Temple and the only Neem Karoli Baba ashram in the West.

Rev. Elizabeth Teal

Rev. Elizabeth Teal specializes in Eco-Theology, the 'human-animal' bond and their connective healing aspects. She is the Spiritual Director for The Ministry of Animals, and the training director for Giving Paws. She graduated *summa cum laude* in Behavioral Science from Mercy College in New York, with additional concentration and studies in animal-assisted therapies. She holds a certificate in Interfaith, Interspiritual Counseling. Her ordination is from and held by One Spirit Interfaith Seminary. Rev. Teal took the vows of the Community of The Mystic Heart in 2010, and reaffirms them every day. She is a mystic, a minister, a chaplain, an artist and a storyteller.

Lynda "Ma Shanti" Terry

Lynda "Ma Shanti" Terry, a CMH Sannyasa Oblate, is an educator, writer, and author of *The 11 Intentions* and its audiobook version, *Invoking the Sacred Feminine as a Pathway to Inner Peace*. She also is a contributor to the award-winning book, *Women, Spirituality and Transformative Leadership: Where Grace Meets Power*. She has taught meditation for more than 25 years, and from 2002-2010 served as founder of an Interspiritual women's peace and service network. She has conducted numerous workshops, classes and retreats on peace embodiment, feminine spirituality, subtle activism and related topics. She also spent more than two decades in the communications field, a goodly portion of that in public relations writing.

CMH's Historic 2016 Retreat in Kentucky

Addendum:
The Five Teachings of Sacred Feet Yoga

The First Teachings
1. *Be as kind to yourself as you are compassionate to others.*
2. *Be as forgiving of yourself as you are generous with others.*
3. *Be as patient with yourself as you are faithful to others.*

The Second Teachings
1. *Trust yourself.*
2. *Trust in your own deep heart.*
3. *Trust in the dance of the universe.*

The Third Teachings
1. *Honor the sacred energy at the core of your being.*
2. *Nurture the Holy Spirit's bright and faithful fire.*
3. *Digest the knowledge that leads unfailingly to freedom.*

The Fourth Teachings
1. *Live your life peacefully—and with purpose.*
2. *Maintain a glad sense of humor.*
3. *Place your faith in stillness, steadiness and service.*

The Fifth Teachings
1. *Be gentle and fair in your dealings.*
2. *Praise others and receive praise graciously.*
3. *Be a courier of faith and wakefulness.*

CPSIA information can be obtained
at www.ICGtesting.com
Printed in the USA
LVOW08s0033160518

577261LV00005B/1007/P